THIS

OUR STORY!

THE STORY OF HUMANITY -
AS TOLD IN THE ANCIENT
SUMERIAN CUNEIFORM CLAY TABLETS!

AND THE MISSING LINK?

Eileen McCourt

This is Our Story!

By Eileen McCourt

This book was first published in Great Britain in paperback during December 2023.

The moral right of Eileen McCourt is to be identified as the author of this work and has been asserted by her in accordance with the Copyright, Designs and Patents Act of 1988.

All rights are reserved and no part of this book may be produced or utilized in any format, or by any means, electronic or mechanical, including photocopying, recording or by any information storage or retrieval system, without prior permission in writing from the publishers - Coast & Country/Ads2life. ads2life@btinternet.com

All rights reserved.

ISBN: 979-8870384160

Copyright © December 2023 Eileen McCourt

CONTENTS

About the Author i

Acknowledgements x

Foreword xi

Chapter 1: Understanding evolution 1

Chapter 2: Visitors from space? 6

Chapter 3: Refuting Darwinism 20

Chapter 4: The 'Cradle of Civilisation' - Mesopotamia, Sumeria, Babylon 50

Chapter 5: Creation according to the ancient Sumerian Cuneiform Clay Tablets 54

    (i) Epic of Atrahasis 77

    (ii) Enuma Elish 86

    (iii) Epic of Gilgamesh 90

Chapter 6: Ancient Babylonian myths 96

    (i) Descent of Inanna 96

    (ii) Myth of Etana 97

    (iii) Myth of Adapa 98

Chapter 7: The Emerald Tablets of Thoth 101

Epilogue: The missing link? 105

Other Books by Eileen McCourt 121

About the Author

Eileen McCourt is a retired school teacher of English and History with a Master's degree in History from University College Dublin.

She is also a Reiki Grand Master teacher and practitioner, having qualified in Ireland, England and Spain, and has introduced many of the newer modalities of Reiki healing energy into Ireland for the first time, from Spain and England. Eileen has qualified in England through the Lynda Bourne School of Enlightenment, and in Spain through the Spanish Federation of Reiki with Alessandra Rossin, Bienstar, Santa Eulalia, Ibiza.

Regular workshops and healing sessions are held in Elysium Wellness, Newry, County Down; New Moon Holistics N.I. Carrickfergus, County Antrim; Angel Times Limerick; Holistic Harmony Omagh, County Tyrone; Celtic School of Sound Healing, Swords, County Dublin; Kingdom Holistic Hub, Mill Road, Killorglin, County Kerry; Reiki Healing Bettystown, County Meath and Moonbeams, Carrigaline County Cork, where Eileen has been teaching the following to both practitioner and teacher levels:

- **Tibetan Usui Reiki levels 1, 2, 3 (Inner Master) 4 (teacher) and Grand Master**

- **Okuna Reiki (Atlantean and Lemurian)**

- **Karuna- Prakriti (Tibetan Usui and Hindu)**

- **Rahanni Celestial Healing**

- **Fire Spirit Reiki (Christ Consciousness and Holy Spirit)**

- Mother Mary Reiki
- Mary Magdalene Reiki
- Archangels Reiki
- Archangels Ascended Masters Reiki
- Reiki Seraphim
- Violet Flame Reiki
- Lemurian Crystal Reiki
- Golden Eagle Reiki (Native North American Indian)
- Golden Chalice Reiki
- Golden Rainbow Ray Reiki
- Goddesses of Light Reiki
- Unicorn Reiki
- Pegasus Reiki
- Elementals Reiki
- Dragon Reiki
- Dolphin Reiki
- Pyramid of Goddess Isis Reiki
- Kundalini Reiki
- Psychic Energy Surgery Healing

Details of all of these modalities can be found on Eileen's website, together with dates and venues of courses and workshops.

This is Eileen's **47th** book.

Previous publications include:

- *'Living the Magic'*, published in December 2014
- *'This Great Awakening'*, September 2015
- *'Spirit Calling! Are You Listening?'*, January 2016
- *'Working With Spirit: A World of Healing'*, January 2016
- *'Life's But A Game! Go With The Flow!'*, March 2016
- *'Rainbows, Angels and Unicorns!'*, April 2016
- *'........And That's The Gospel Truth!'*, September 2016
- *'The Almost Immaculate Deception! The Greatest Scam in History?'*, September 2016
- *'Are Ye Not Gods?' The true inner meanings of Jesus' teachings and messages'*, March 2017
- *'Jesus Lost and Found'*, July 2017
- *'Behind Every Great Man........ Mary Magdalene Twin Flame of Jesus'*, July 2017
- *'Out of the Mind and into the Heart: Our Spiritual Journey with Mary Magdalene'*, August 2017
- *'Divinely Designed: The Oneness of the Totality of ALL THAT IS'*, January 2018. Also in **Audiobook**, May 2019

- *'Resurrection or Resuscitation? What really happened in That Tomb?',* May 2018

- *'Music of the Spheres: Connecting to the Great Universal Consciousness and to ALL THAT IS through the music of Irish composer/pianist Pat McCourt',* June 2018

- *'Chakras, Crystals, Colours and Drew the Dragon: A child's second Spiritual book',* July 2018

- *'The Voice of a Master: It is Jesus Himself Who Speaks: Know Thyself',* December 2018

- *'Kundalini',* January 2019

- *'Brave Little Star Child Comes To Earth'* - Audiobook- April 2019

- *'The Truth will set you free. - Christianity: Where did it all begin?'* May 2019

- *'Titus Flavius Josephus: Did Josephus write the gospels?'* June 2019

- *'Homo SPACIENS: We Are Not From Planet Earth! Our connection with UFOs, ETs and Ancient Civilisations'* August 2019

- *'Those Strange Looking Men In Their Flying Machines: Visitors From Beyond Time and Space? Or From Planet Earth? - ETs, UFOs and Who Knows What'* September 2019

- *'I Want to Break Free: Helping our Planet Earth ascend to a higher vibration of Love, Joy, Peace and Happiness for all. We can do it!'* November 2019

- *'The Universe is Mental! Understanding the 7 Spiritual Laws of the Universe, the Hermetic Principles that govern Creation'* January 2020

- *'To Be Or Not To Be.... The Man of Stratford who was never to be Shakespeare: Exposing the deception that was William Shakespeare'* February 2020

- *'If Not Shakespeare, Then Who? Unmasking the Real Bard of Avon! '* April 2020

- *'What On Earth Is Happening? 2020: Year of Balance: Rise of the Divine Feminine'* April 2020

- *'Creating a New World! - Nature WILL be obeyed! - The greatest lesson never taught, but which we need to learn'* May 2020

- *'Humanity's Greatest Challenge? Breaking out of the vortex of ignorance and superstition'* May 2020

- *'Puppets on a String! But! The Strings have been broken! We are free!'* July 2020

- *'Out of the Darkness of Deception and Despair - into the Light of Truth',* February 2021

- *'Lighting the Way: A Little Magic Book of Spiritual Messages and Meanings',* May 2021

- *'Man in the Mirror: Reality or Illusion?'* July 2021

- *'Living Earth: Our Relationship with Mother Nature',* July 2021

- 'The Singing Soul', July 2021

- 'Finding Sense in the Non-Sense: Seeing the greater picture', September 2021

- 'Above Our Heads: Predators or Protectors? Extraterrestrials; - The best-kept secret now exposed? - January 2022

- 'Changing your life - Living the Reiki Way - In Today's World! Just for Today...' January 2022

- 'Dear God.......Where are you?......A Bewildered Soul Talks With God' - February 2022

- 'You're just a number....and the Universe has it! ' May 2022

- 'Let Eriu Remember - Lessons and teachings embedded in myths and legends of our sacred sites' . - November 2022

- 'Ancient Ancestors Calling! With words of wisdom and knowledge for today's world'.   - December 2022

- Wake Up! This is it! The Great Apocalypse! - There is nothing hidden that will not be revealed'. - May 2023

- 'The Simulator. Are we living in a simulation? Are we trapped? If so, how do we escape?'

- 'The Soul Net! Does it exist? Are we a trawling ground for energy vampires and other-worldly parasites? How do we avoid getting caught?'

and now this current book: 'This Is Our Story! The Story of Humanity - as Told in the Ancient Sumerian Cuneiform Clay Tablets! - And the Missing Link?'

Podcasts for each of these 47 books can be viewed on Eileen's website and on her author page.

Eileen has also just recently re-published a series of 5 local history books under the title '*Finding Our Way Back*'. These were first published in the 1980s:

Book One: '*Strange Happenings*' - a 1988 collection of local ghost stories and local cures and charms, collected by the students of Saint Patrick's College Armagh.

Book Two: '*Tell Me More, Grandad!*' - a collection of school day memories collected from grandparents and great-grandparents in 1990.

Book Three: '*Gather In, Gather In*', - a collection of children's games and rhymes, 1942-1943, by the late Mr. Paddy Hamill, collected from the pupils in Lislea No 2 Primary School 1939 to 1947 when Mr. Hamill was Principal.

Book Four: '*A Peep Into The Past: Armagh in Great-Granny's day*' - Earlier maps of Armagh, explaining how Armagh got its street names, together with photographs of streets and shop-fronts in the early 20th century. Also included is information on schools and education in Armagh in the 19th Century; newspaper articles of interest from 1848; traders in Armagh in 1863 and markets and fairs in Armagh, - of which there were many!

Book Five: "*The Poor Law And The Workhouse In Armagh 1838-1948*' - prepared when Eileen was on secondment in the Public Record Office of Northern Ireland, 1980-1981, under the scholarship scheme provided for teachers by the Department of Education. The resulting publication was used in local schools for coursework for examination purposes. Primary sources include the Armagh workhouse registers and minute books, which are all held in the Northern Ireland Public Record Office in Belfast; government commissions and reports; annual reports of the Poor Law Commission for Ireland 1847-1921, and photographs of the inside and outside of Armagh workhouse, now part of Tower Hill Hospital, taken in 1989 by the late Mary Donnelly (nee Finn), Saint Patrick's College, Armagh.

The recent series of FB weekly videos, **'Our Great Awakening'**, together with the previous series **'The Nature of........'** with Eileen and Declan Quigley, Shamanic practitioner and teacher can also be viewed on Eileen's website and on YouTube, together with a series of healing meditations and Shamanic journeys.

Recent Full Moon Meditations with Declan Quigley, Jennifer Maddy and Brenda Murnaghan can be viewed on Eileen's YouTube channel, - access through website.

Eileen has also recorded 6 guided meditation CDs with her brother, composer/pianist Pat McCourt:

- **'Celestial Healing'**
- **'Celestial Presence'**
- **'Cleansing, energising and balancing the Chakras'**
- **'Ethereal Spirit' - Meditation on the 'I Am Presence'**
- **'Open the Door to Archangel Michael'**
- **'Healing with Archangel Raphael'**

Eileen's first DVD, '*Living the Magic' features* a live interview in which Eileen talks about matters Spiritual.

All publications are available from Amazon online and all publications and CDs are in Angel and Holistic centres around the country, as specified on website.

Please visit also the BLOG page on Eileen's website.

Website: www.celestialhealing8.co.uk

Author page: www.eileenmccourt.co.uk

YouTube channel:

https://www.youtube.com/channel/UChJPprUDnI9Eeu0IrRjGsqw

ACKNOWLEDGEMENTS

Book number **47!**

Thank you yet again to my publishers Dr. Steve Green and Don Hale OBE, for all their work and support, and without whom none of these books would ever actually materialise!

And of course, not forgetting all of you who are buying my books and CDs wherever in the world you are, and all who have taken the time to give me feed-back, and to write reviews for me, both in my books and on Amazon. You are greatly appreciated!

Thank you to all who attend my courses, workshops and meditation sessions, sharing your amazing energies, taking us on such wonderful journeys and through such amazing experiences! We are all so blessed!

And thank you to all of you who have been following me on Facebook. I sincerely hope the posts are bringing some comfort and help to you in these present rapidly changing times when so many people are paralysed with fear, anxiety and uncertainty.

But all is well! All is as it should be! The Earth and all in her and on her are moving into a higher energy vibration level - all are ascending! So hold on! Don't give up! Not now! Not now when we have already come so far!

And as always, I give thanks for all the great blessings that are constantly being sent our way in this wonderful, loving, abundant universe.

Namaste!

1st January 2024

FOREWORD

Today, at this time of what we call the Great Apocalypse, meaning time of great revelations, the amount of information tumbling out to us in free fall is nothing short of a tsunami, even a deluge. Numerous television documentaries on the History and Discovery Channels, together with archaeological discoveries such as equinox and solar alignments in ancient stone circles, megalithic structures, the unearthing of hidden ancient texts and scrolls, - including the Sumerian Cuneiform Tablets, - the Epic of Gilgamesh, the Atrahasis Myth, the Eunan Elish, - the Babylonian Tablets, the Emerald Tablets, the Book of Enoch, the Nag Hammadi Gospels, the Vedas, to name just a few, - these are all contributing to, and fuelling this great awakening that humanity is experiencing right now. All explaining to us that long ago, in a distant past, advanced civilisations, far in advance of us, once existed on Earth and were, with the passing of time, destroyed by devastating global cataclysm, - and yes! - according to some of these same ancient cuneiform tablets, and if these ancient tablets are indeed to be believed, - by nuclear war!

Are the origins of humanity really what we have been taught, and just because that is what we have been taught, we assume it all to be true?

How would you feel if you found out that everything you had ever been taught was not the truth? All a deliberate lie? Truth and knowledge kept from us, key evidence withheld, to serve some particular agenda?

George Orwell's famous quote from his justifiably famous fiction novel *'Nineteen Eighty-Four'* comes to mind:

'Who controls the past controls the future: who controls the present controls the past'.

In other words, should we be considering how the past determines our future? To predict the future, to foresee what is coming, should we look to the past? Is history just repeating itself in a cyclical manner?

Certainly, if we do not know about and understand our past, then we are doomed to repeat it. Surely the higher goal of studying and learning about history is that it should ultimately teach us not to repeat humanity's past mistakes? But we do indeed appear to be going around in circles! Learning nothing from history! So would this not very strongly suggest that we have been very cleverly conditioned? Conditioned by a very tightly controlled historical narrative? Conditioned to accept and believe all that we have been told by those supposedly *'leading experts'* in their field? Conditioned to not question or not search for alternative theories?

All that we have been told and taught about ancient history and the history of mankind, - we have trusted in it all! But! Have we ever been taught through our education systems in school about what really matters, - the nature of reality; sentient life in the universe; energy and how it works; the secrets of consciousness; who we are; from where we have come; where we are going, and our place in the universe and in the cosmos?

We have indeed been force-fed and drip-fed a very limited and exclusive diet of only what those in power want us to know. And of course, history is written by the winners! Spin, Spin, Spin! Propaganda, Propaganda, Propaganda! All euphemised and dressed up in the name of politics!

that holds the key to understanding the origins of creation and of man? Ancient knowledge that we are not supposed to find? Ancient knowledge cleverly hidden and concealed within certain secret societies and elite families, - all kept from us to keep us in the lower third dimension energy level of Planet Earth? The higher levels of energy and consciousness awareness blocked from us, keeping us trapped in the chains and fetters of the material world? Why is all that information so guarded? We need to ask!

But there is nothing hidden that will not be revealed! And whatever secrets are hidden within government secret files and in Vatican secret vaults and libraries will eventually come to light! And that is one thing of which we can be certain, - in a world where so much continues to defy any sort of logic and where there continues to be so much uncertainty.

And in these ancient documents, we read about such places as the Planet Nibiri, the ancient civilisations of Atlantis and Lemuria, and such other-worldly beings as Anu, Enki, Elil, Marduk, the Anunnaki, - just some of those who, and again I emphasise, - according to the ancient texts, - came here to our Planet Earth, for various reasons, from various parts of the cosmic zodiac, and who, according to these same ancient texts, were responsible for the origins of humanity! Those who have been responsible for genetically engineering and moderating our human DNA, - for whatever purpose! Those advanced, intelligent extraterrestrial beings who visited and perhaps even colonised Earth. And in the process, '*upgraded*' the primitive Homo Erectus by means of genetic engineering to create Homo Sapiens, - humanity as we know it. Homo Sapiens! A hybrid being, incorporating a mix of terrestrial genes from Homo Erectus and extraterrestrial genes from an alien cosmic species, an ancient civilisation, seen as a race of '*gods*' descending from the sky in their chariot-like vehicles.

So, have we been made in the '*likeness of God*' or in the '*likeness of the gods?*'

'*God*' with a capital '*G*' or '*gods*' with a small '*g*'?

The '*gods*' here being plural, - those strange-looking saucer men depicted on ancient tombs and cave walls thousands of years ago, all descending from the sky in various forms of spacecraft or chariots, and who so strongly resemble our modern-day astronauts!

And again, as in all my previous books, I cannot tell you what to believe! I can only present certain information, - whether that information be just too unbelievable, too incredible, too fantastical to be acceptable, - but it is up to each and every person to process that information for himself.

The main request I make however is, that in the processing of all this information on an individual basis, we each keep an open mind on absolutely everything. It is because of our closed minds that we are in the mess we are in at this present time. We have been swallowing wholesale everything that has been presented to us as truth, remaining unwilling to upset the proverbial apple cart! And it is easier for us to accept what other people tell us, people whom we believe are working for us in our best interest, rather than to have to investigate for ourselves! But that is just handing over responsibility to others! And we all have a responsibility to find out the truth! The proverbial ostrich act no longer works! We need to get our heads out of the sand!

Do your own research! Do **not** just take my word for anything!

And in doing your own research, prepare to be shocked! Just as I was! The initial shock and disbelief, however, is all part of the process of liberation! The process of becoming liberated and free! Because with the truth comes liberation and freedom! The truth will indeed set you free!

And in doing your own research, you will unearth the story of humanity, - **'Our Story',** which is what this book is all about.

Chapter 1:

Understanding evolution

When we think of the word evolution, and the evolution of humanity, we tend to think of the ***physical evolving*** of the human race, - whether from the apes, selective evolution, the big bang, or from whatever.

BUT! We are not just physical beings! To see ourselves as such is extremely limiting! As eternal consciousness, we are first and foremost spiritual beings. Spiritual beings having a physical experience. And our physical body is only the vehicle, the means through which we are able to experience our temporary physicality. I am not this white, brown, black or whatever-colour body. I am not this poor, wealthy, healthy, disabled, or whatever-condition body. I am a spiritual being encased in this temporary body for the duration of this life-time only.

And in this life-time, and only on this third dimension energy vibration level we call Planet Earth, we experience that which we call time. And that which we call time is abstract, a concept, a demarcating factor solely for this earth vibration energy frequency.

In just the same way as life is our experience of reality at a particular energetic level, so too, time is also experiential. Time is relative and flexible and, according to Albert Einstein himself, time, "*the dividing line between past, present, and future is an illusion*". Planet Earth is enveloped in a time warp, but a time warp which plays a vital part in our soul evolution and the raising of the collective spiritual consciousness of all humanity. Time, as we know it, simply brings structure and order to our earth dimension.

Time divides all our experiences up into the past, present and future, for the simple purpose of affording humanity the time needed to learn the lessons we need to learn in order to progress upwards to the higher spiritual energy frequencies and to eventually attain Mastery. To quote Pythagoras:

'Time is the soul of this world.'

Time apparently only exists on evolving planets, in order to assist its species in learning the lesson that we are all One in the total Oneness of the Great Universal God Energy, the lesson that all life is inter-connected, inter-twined and inter-dependent. It is only on evolving planets, such as earth, that there is separation or demarcation by time or space.

Time does not speed up as we grow older. In fact time has nothing to do with growing older. What speeds time up is not the number of earth years we clock up, but how we **grow or expand in consciousness**, how we grow or expand in increasing awareness of what and who we are, why we are here and our place in the infinity of creation. We are all beings of light, and the higher up the different energy levels in the Spirit world we reach, then the lighter we become. Time ceases to exist. That is our reality!

It is the growth of only our physical body that has all got to do with time, - linear time which is a feature only of this third dimension energy vibration level we call Planet Earth.

And while we grow in our physical body through linear time, we grow or expand in consciousness, in spiritual awareness, through increasing our awareness of what and who we really are, why we are here, and our place in the infinity and entirety of Creation.

So the real meaning of evolution lies in the raising of our human awareness, our human consciousness, to higher states of spiritual consciousness. That is the reason why we are here! To raise our own spiritual consciousness and the collective spiritual consciousness of all humanity. To assist humanity towards full Ascension! In the words of Lao Tzu, the semi-legendary sixth century BCE Chinese philosopher, credited with founding the philosophical system of Taoism:

'The key to growth is the introduction of higher dimensions of consciousness into our awareness.'

But we have lost sight of all of this! We have become so caught up in the physical trappings of our life here that we have forgotten our real mission in life. We have become obsessed with attaining wealth and material possessions, judging how successful each of us is by the amount of wealth we have managed to accrue, the number of letters after our name, the qualifications we have managed to achieve. And living at this level means we are still firmly in the third dimension energy frequency level.

And the reason why our world is suffering so much right now is because not enough people are on a high enough level of consciousness. We are constantly being dragged back down again to this lower state of consciousness by all the negative energy forces surrounding us. Our evolution process appears to have been stalled or even thwarted!

The problems in our current world are neither basically political nor economic! Our problem is a spiritual problem! We are caught in a consciousness trap! The consciousness trap where we believe we are separate individuals paddling our own proverbial canoe in a world where we believe only the fittest can survive.

We are all of the same substance! And not only are we **of** the same substance, - we **are** the same substance.

And yes, at the same time as **being the same substance**, each and every one of us is unique in our own individual being. Uniqueness in diversity! It is indeed meaningless to view any one of us as a separate entity as everything in creation is in a continuing and changing flow of energy. We are all the same thing, all the same stuff, in an unbroken cycle, all in the one enormous infinite something, all an inherent part of the **ONE** undivided whole, part of a continuum.

Vaclav Havel, former president of Czechoslovakia wrote:

'Without a global revolution in consciousness, nothing will change for the better.........and the catastrophe towards which this world is headed ----- the ecological, social, demographic, or general breakdown of civilization - will be unavoidable.'

The only way humanity can evolve is by raising the collective human consciousness to higher vibrational levels of energy. To the consciousness level where we see the **ONENESS** of **ALL THAT IS.** To the consciousness level where we see that everything and everyone is within each and every one of us, and each and every one of us is within everything and everyone else. Just as in the hologram! Cut a holographic image up into tiny pieces, and the entire holographic image is still retained within each and every tiny part. The macrocosm contained within the microcosm.

Each one of us is a microcosm of the macrocosm of **ALL THAT IS.**

And coming into a realisation, an acknowledgement and an acceptance of this is what is truly meant by the *evolution* of humanity! And in order to evolve as a species, we have to get ourselves out of this trap of consciousness! This trap of consciousness of limiting third dimension thinking and seeing that this is preventing our evolution into the higher energy vibration frequency levels. Our *evolution* into higher states of consciousness - the true meaning of *evolution*!

Chapter 2:

Visitors from space?

Erich von Däniken is recognised by millions from his regular appearances on television history channels in the **'Ancient Aliens'** series, and from his forty-plus published books, the main content of which is his assertion and profound belief that extraterrestrials have been visiting our Planet Earth for thousands of years.

It was Erich von Däniken who made famous **the ancient aliens** theory, and the theory of **ancient astronauts**. He has travelled far and wide around the globe to study the many strange phenomena that he concludes all point to the one conclusion - that many thousands of years ago the earth was visited by a race of superhuman powers and intelligence. His books certainly present powerful evidence of our extraterrestrial ancestors. He has devoted years of his life to studying unsolved mysteries of the past.

His first book, *'Chariots of the Gods', 1968,* which sold in millions, provoked a worldwide storm of controversy. It produced a massive shift in human consciousness and awareness at a time when minds were opening, changing humanity's view of the cosmos on a massive scale. In the era of the space race, Von Däniken proclaimed that earth had been visited by more advanced beings early in our history. But pre-scientific man had no concept of spaceships, so he called their vehicles '*chariots*' and so those driving the chariots became '*gods*'.

Von Däniken challenges his readers:

'How often the pillars of our wisdom have crumpled into dust! Hundreds and hundreds of generations thought that the earth was flat. The iron law that the sun went round the earth held good for thousands of years. We are still convinced that our earth is the centre of everything, although it has been proved that the earth is an ordinary star of insignificant size, 30,000 light years from the centre of the Milky Way.

The time has come for us to admit our insignificance by making discoveries in the infinite unexplored cosmos. Only then shall we realise that we are nothing but ants in the vast State of the universe.' (Erich von Däniken, *'Chariots of the Gods'* page 18)

Von Däniken points to all the fantastic ancient ruins across the world, and maintains they cannot be explained by conventional theories of history, archaeology and religion. Sites and ruins such as for example, the Moai Statues on Easter Island, off the west coast of South America; Stonehenge in Southern England; Avebury in South West England; Sacsayhuamán Fortress-Temple Complex near Cuzco, in the Andes in Peru; the Carnac Stones in Brittany in North West France; the Black Pagoda in Konark in India, also known as the Temple of the Sun Konark; the Baalbek Platform in Eastern Lebanon; the Zimbabwe Ruins in Rhodesia; the Nazca Lines in Peru and, - nearer home, Newgrange here in Ireland and all the ancient megalithic stone circles dotted around our country.

And why, Von Däniken asks, for instance, do the world's sacred books describe gods who came down from the sky in fiery chariots and always promised to return? How could an ancient Sanskrit text contain an account which could only be of a journey in an alien craft? And he compares photographs of American space centre launch sites to the constructions on the plains of Nazca in Peru. And in order to understand these mysteries which Däniken has catalogued, he insists that we must go back to these ancient sites with an open mind.

Anyone who tunes in regularly to Sky Television's Discovery, History and Science Channels will no doubt be aware of the recently increased number of documentary programmes dealing with ancient civilisations, aliens, extraterrestrials and various unexplained phenomena. Learned and reputable people are presenting us with very convincing material and evidence on a constant and on-going basis, material that must surely force us to re-think. **'Ancient Aliens'** began in 2009, and over 200 episodes have now been broadcast on History Channel, with new information and some on repeat, due to public demand. It has now, and for the last number of years, got the highest viewing figures in the history of the History Channel.

These television documentaries are all showing the strong possibility that extraterrestrial forces have been visiting us here on Planet Earth for centuries upon centuries, teaching us their skills in an effort to help us progress on our spiritual path. They suggest that great minds such as Leonardo da Vinci in the Middle Ages were in some sort of communication or correspondence with extraterrestrial beings. These extraterrestrial beings who were instilling into Da Vinci's mind the great inventions that he came up with. For example, his plans for a helicopter. Was there some greater, more advanced being from beyond our physical earth realm instructing him?

But what about lesser known people?

Otto O. Binder is a distinguished science writer, specialising in space and the UFO phenomena. He is the author of ten books and has written numerous science-fact articles for national magazines. He has also written under contract for NASA. He is an active member of various aerospace, rocketry, aeronautics and astronautics associations.

In his book 'Ancient Aliens And Other Unsolved Mysteries Of The Past', Binder writes:

'During the Renaissance, dozens of less well-known professional people mathematicians, surgeons, historians, physicists, astronomers - wrote treatises in which visiting beings held conversations with them and aided them in discovering new scientific principles.' (Otto Binder, 'Ancient Aliens' page 69-70)

And the reason for all this intervention by extraterrestrials? Why were they apparently so determined to help humanity?

'If the earth is the saucermen's colony, the logic is inescapable. After the fall of the Roman Empire, mankind had been thrown into the Dark Ages for a thousand years. The saucermen kept hoping we would pull out of it ourselves, or perhaps what help our star-sires tried to give was rejected as witchcraft and heresy.

After a grave conclave, perhaps the saucermen launched a concerted effort to end this period of unenlightenment before their space-spawned civilization on earth blinked out altogether and degenerated into savagery.

So they began landings en masse, each with a target - some bright men who would listen to them and benefit by the knowledge. Through maybe for a century or two, the saucermen had to work hard on key men, giving them the inspirations that made geniuses in history. Galileo, Copernicus, Newton, da Vinci, Pascal, Pasteur, Volta, Hertz,

Descartes - any or all of these shining intellects may possibly have had the unseen aid of the starmen, to push science ahead and revive civilization.' (Otto Binder, *'Ancient Aliens'* page 70)

Even if we make the most fleeting or briefest examination of ancient civilisations we will find stories of strange beings that came down from the heavens to interact with mankind and provide them with technology, religion and knowledge, before returning again to their home amongst the stars. Despite this, history tends to assume that these legends are simply myths. However, considering modern stories of UFOs and alleged alien contact, there are startling similarities between recent UFO encounters and ancient accounts. The only difference is that early man had no real concept of the reality of life on other planets. To them, strange beings coming down from the sky in glowing chariots were understood to be gods, angels, or demons. They knew nothing else. In the same way, when the railway was built across America and the native peoples saw it for the first time, they described it, in their limited language and without knowing anything about mechanical devices, as *'horses of steel'*. That was all they knew.

In a time before the development of the written word or spoken language, ancient man painted scenes of their lives on outside rock walls or on the ceilings and walls of caves. This artwork often shows wild animals and sometimes people. But, all across the planet, prehistoric art also depicts strange objects and unusual humanoid creatures that do not appear to be part of the natural environment. Many ancient illustrations and stone sculptures depict figures in strange attire for the times and sporting unusual headgear like we know modern day astronauts to wear. Could they really be evidence of ancient alien astronauts, ancient visitors from space? Ancient visitors from other worlds beyond our Planet Earth, inter-galactic, interdimensional beings touching down on earth, - for whatever reason?

C.R. Hale is the editor of *'Ancient Aliens, Written Supplement: Chariots, Gods and Beyond',* a compilation of ancient alien theory literature and transcripts to provide readers with an overview of the viewpoints of key proponents to the ancient alien theory. Hale has carefully built a collection of material that complements the topics introduced in the popular TV series *'Ancient Aliens'* with material from all the main contributors to the series, including Erich von Däniken, Giorgio Tsoukalos, David Childress, Michael Cremo, Jason Martell and others. Hale writes:

'These people witnessed something. They were told something. And they tried to depict it the best they could with the kind of technology they had at the time. And that was simple tools and simple artwork..........

You know, pictures are worth a thousand words, absolutely. When you see pictures depicted for example, on a cave in Italy that shows two astronauts with helmets on, what the heck could it be?' (George Noory, Radio host, Coast to Coast AM) (Quoted from *'Ancient Aliens, Written Supplement'*, edited by C.R. Hale, page 44 and 45)

The internet and Wikipedia the free encyclopedia provide many and various examples of ancient art depicting visitors from space, and vast information is accessible to everyone at the click of a button.

For instance, we find that 29,000-year-old cave paintings in Tanzania depict several disc-shaped objects that appear to be hovering over the landscape. Another painting shows four humanoid entities surrounding a woman while another looks down from the sky from inside some sort of box.

In northern Australia, there are a number of 5,000-year-old cave paintings that show strange beings with large heads and eyes, wearing spacesuit-like garments. The Aborigines said that these creatures, called Wandjina, came down from the Milky Way during the Dreamtime and created the Earth and all its inhabitants.

Ancient Egyptian legends tell of the *'First Time'*, which is described as an age when sky gods came down to earth and raised the land from the mud and water. They supposedly traveled through the air in flying boats and brought laws and wisdom to man through a royal line of pharaohs.

And Otto Binder tells us:

'The Indians of North America still today repeat an ancient story which Longfellow immortalized in his poem 'Hiawatha', of a Red Swan that was also like a sun that descended to earth and brought the Son of the Evening Star, a spaceman, who created humanity.

On an Egyptian papyrus the Pharaoh Thutmose III about 1504-1450 B.C.E., had his scribe write down that witnesses saw 'a circle of fire that was coming down from the sky......Its body was one rod long and one rod wide......'

Several days later, the account goes on, the objects became numerous in the sky, shining more brightly than the sun. The full text gives the distinct impression that they were observing glowing or fiery craft maneuvering in the sky.

Many scholars and writers believe that the Grecian and Roman gods of Olympus were in reality skymen (spacemen) whose supernatural powers were really super-scientific in nature, and that these tales go back thousands of years to when the skymen came to earth to create and nurture the human race.

Egyptian hieroglyphics as far back as 4500 B.C.E. credit their god, Osiris, for coming down from an 'island in the sky' and teaching agriculture to struggling, nomadic mankind, so that stable civilization could begin.

From India and its civilization of 5000 B.C.E., Sanskrit writings prove a fertile source of UFO-oriented legends, which are divided into mythical and factual events. Among the events scripts is this straightforward passage: 'By means of these machines, human beings can fly in the air and heavenly beings can come down to earth'.

Peruvian legend allegorically claims that their first people were born from bronze, gold and silver eggs which had fallen from heaven.' (Otto Binder, *'Ancient Aliens* page 84-85)

Other ancient legends, which seem to refer to the fabled Atlantis, describe a vimanas craft: *'the beautiful car-celestial possessed the radiance of fire....'*

And of special relevance for this book, Clay tablets inscribed around 2,600 BC by the ancient Sumerians detail a 400,000-year history that included visits by creatures called Anunnaki, who flew in vehicles called Shems. These celestial craft were described as being tall, rocket-like *'rocks'* which emitted fire. The Sumerians never called the Anunnaki *'gods'* but rather *'dingir',* meaning *'righteous ones of the bright pointed objects'.*

And referring again to Erich von Däniken:

'The Shillah tribe in southern Sudan say that the first human being,

Omara, had originally come from heaven. At that time, humans still lived like wild animals and killed one another. But Omara weaned them away from the animals and taught them everything they needed to know. Omara had also founded the first kingdom on Earth....

Always the same: The original teachers always came from the stars. The Nuba tribe lives primarily in the middle of Sudan and forms the largest non-Arab group. They are a group of more than a million people, which nevertheless speak different languages. All of them have the creation myth in common according to which the heavenly god Nuba ordered his divine messenger Su to bring grain to humans.......the divine messenger showed humans the grain and taught them how to make fields and grow cereals.' (Erich von Däniken, *'The Gods Never Left Us'*, page 152)

'I wrote extensively about the Dogon tribe in the Republic of Mali, in my last book. Their heavenly teacher was called Nomo and came from the constellation of Sirius. This Nomo also told the Dogo about the Sirius system. He explained to them that Sirius was a dual star (currently Sirius A+B) and that there were still additional celestial bodies in the system (which are still unknown to our astronomers).' (Erich von Däniken, *'The Gods Never Left Us'*, page 153)

"*South American peoples, including the Inca and Warao tribes, even say that originally humans had lived in heaven and had descended from time to time to hunt here. It was only later that they settled here. But they had sporadically been visited again and taught by their heavenly ancestors. Reports of the same kind can be found among the Kogi Indians in Colombia. They live in the mountains on the Caribbean side of Colombia, their original heavenly teachers created the first humans, instructed them in all matters, and continue to visit them* *today. It was the same teachers who warned human beings thousands of years ago about a flood which would be intentionally caused and ordered them to build ships. 'And the priests, the older brothers, all descended from heaven'........ That is astonishing for a lateral thinker like myself, for the same story was told worlds and oceans away from Colombia. The Sumerian King List <WB444>, currently in the British Museum in London, says, 'After the flood had passed, the Kingdom descended from heaven once more'. And the same is told in the Gilgamesh epic, which also originates from Sumer. After the flood, the gods descended from the heavens'. "* (Erich von Däniken, *'The Gods Never Left Us'*, page 154)

'Who would have the courage to ignore this worldwide accumulation of statements? In what age are we living? In the 17th century or the age of global communications?' (Erich von Däniken, *'The Gods Never Left Us'*, page 154)

'The Tatoosh native peoples on the northwest coast of California not only report about a 'Thunderbird', which descended from the heavens and instructed their ancestors, but they also still represent the Thunderbird on their totem poles today. The Hopi in Arizona.... know about the heavenly teachers and naturally venerate these teachers in the form of dolls.........Naturally the Kayapo on the upper Amazon, 8,000 kilometers distant from the Hopik, know the same thing and celebrate it in their dances even today.' (Erich von Däniken, *'The Gods Never Left Us'*, page 155)

'And how do we act? We continue to live in the dulled, sticky mess of the psychology of religion, which has answers to everything, none of which are true.' (Erich von Däniken, *'The Gods Never Left Us'*, page 155)

'The Japanese tribe of the Yamasachi tells of a time 'when there were still demigods who commuted between heaven and Earth as they wished'.......... The Baltic Latvian people....their principal god was called Dievs. Dievs lived in heaven and ruled there over vast riches. He rode around the heavenly mountain on his flying horse and, at the time of the terrestrial harvest, descended from heaven to earth.......Chinese mythology is familiar with nine heavens, whereby the supreme heavenly god resided in the constellation of the Great Bear. The original emperors reached the earth with fire-breathing dragons. In the Tibetan highlands, it is not just the first ruler, Gesar, who came from space but also many other gods. And how? 'Heaven resounded, the earth shook, there was the roaring of dragons'. The quote could come from the Old Testament. But it doesn't. It comes from Tibetan mythology. Other heavenly beings of Tibet 'used a rope or ladder to descend......Many sons of gods descend from the heaven of the gods to the earth of humans. They then become the rulers and kings of human beings.' (Erich von Däniken, *The Gods Never Left Us*, page 160)

'The Bantu tribe in Cameroon tells of its oldest patriarch that he flew down to their tribal homeland in a large hollowed-out tree. 'Everything we can see was made by Mubei. First he made the earth........then the grass steppes.......then put the animals on them...... Nyoenduma made a great rock rain. Whereupon it opened with great thunder and brought forth the first two humans.' (Erich von Däniken, *The Gods Never Left Us*, page 154)

'Terra del Fuego, the southern tip of South America, is poles apart from Tibet. Like everywhere else, the primal human being, Kenos, came to earth to bring order to it. 'Then he flew back to heaven; he now lives among the stars'. (Erich von Däniken, *The Gods Never Left Us*, page 160)

So what can we conclude from all of this?

Certainly, as Otto Binder says:

'Many parts of history may some day have to be rewritten, if and when our saucermen make themselves known and tell of their unheralded doings in human affairs since ancient times.' (Otto Binder, 'Ancient Aliens' page 70)

'Only one thing seems reasonably certain - that they are extraterrestrial beings, but not necessarily from one world. Among scientific authorities, despite their aversion to mentioning the verboten flying saucers or UFOs, nevertheless they speculate on purely astronomical or cosmological grounds about other-world civilizations and earth's place in this vast community of intelligent life interspersed throughout the galaxy.' (Otto Binder, 'Ancient Aliens' page 107)

'Leaping from the remote past to the present, the signs that the saucermen are still here observing us, and in greater numbers than in the past, are very numerous. Yet they do not necessarily travel back and forth from some headquarters hundreds of thousands of light-years away. They may have nearby bases..........What could be more convenient for them in their watchdog activities over their earth colony, than to have bases on the moon, only 240,000 miles away?.........To them this would be a mere hop done regularly and with some ease, compared to the enormous trip from their home star.' (Otto Binder, 'Ancient Aliens' page 159)

So let us end this chapter with a few opinions from some of those whom we see regularly on our television screens in the Discovery and History channels:

'When all of these stories were written down, writing was a fairly new invention. The very first thing they wrote down is something that actually happened to them, it was so important, so compelling, so significant to them that they had to put it in writing. Why can't modern society come to grips that these stories might be true after all? ....

And the crazy thing is that all of those stories are totally accepted in the modern society of India............

'I got to tell you this. I would be out of a job in India, because there if I were to talk about Ancient Aliens and ancient gods, they would say, 'Okay, so what else is new?............

All over the world we have statues and sculptures and paintings and depictions of these extraterrestrials beings. Even in the United States at Sego Canyon, Utah, we have petroglyphs of very weird-looking creatures that have antennae on their heads, helmets. And halfway around the world in Kimberley, Australia, for example, we have the exact same depictions of these helmeted beings with a halo around their heads. And the question I have is: what did our ancestors see that compelled them to put this on their cave walls? On yet another continent, in Guatemala City, we have a sculpture that looks eerily reminiscent of a modern-day astronaut. I mean, that thing is wearing a helmet. There is some type of a mouthpiece. And on his chest are some type of controls or a breathing apparatus. How is this possible 1,500 years ago? And in Columbia, there were thousands of tomb artifacts that look like modern day airplanes. It has fixed wings, it has a fuselage, and it has an upright tailfin, which is not intrinsic to nature, but is intrinsic to modern-day astrodynamics. Did our ancestors see something similar flying in the air? Absolutely. Another compelling artifact that was found was at the Istanbul Museum, where you have this headless spaceman sitting inside some type of a space vehicle. You can see his hands and you can see tubing that go to some sort of devices. He's wearing a suit. His legs are crammed in there. I mean, even to the untrained eye, this looks very aerodynamic and it looks something that, you know, came from outer space' (Giorgio E. Tsoukalos, publisher 'Legendary Times Magazine')

'Were they just mythological tales that they were making up, fantasy? Or are these physical, real events, and they were trying to describe them as the best that they could? That seems to make more sense to me.' (Jason Martell, '*Knowledge Apocalypse*')

'Many of these ancient civilizations were widely separated in space and time. They weren't in communication with each other. But still, they have the same kind of accounts. I think it's because they all experienced these things and they all have the idea that we're part of a cosmic hierarchy of beings. So, I think, we can't explain things so easily.' (Michael Cremo, author '*Forbidden Archaeology*')

So! Visitors from space? Decide for yourself!

Chapter 3:

Refuting Darwinism

Men are from Mars, Women are from Venus'. The title of John Gray's well-known book! But there is a deeper, more poignant meaning behind this iconic title! And that meaning? - That none of us, neither man nor woman amongst us, is actually from here on Planet Earth!

So, from where have we come? Who are we? Where did humanity originate?

Down through history, as we humans here on Planet Earth considered ourselves and our world to be the center of the universe, and when we were ignorant of any other form of intelligent life outside of our own planet, then it was probably natural for us to believe that the origins of man lay within our planet. To our knowledge, there was just no other place from where humans could have come. Turning to space to find the origins of life was just unthinkable, even considered extreme heresy. So the story of Adam and Eve was part of the belief system of many, as was Charles Darwin's theory of natural selective evolution and humanity descending from the apes. And that is the key word - **theory**! We have lots of theories - the theory of the Big Bang, for example, or the theory of the dinosaurs being wiped out by a meteorite. But they are just theories! Not proven facts! Simply mere speculation!

And the Darwinian Theory? The Darwinian Theory of selective evolution? The Darwinian Theory that has been believed as the explanation for the origins of humanity. The Darwinian **theory** of evolution!

The very same Darwinian **theory** of evolution that Dr. Thomas Henry Huxley of the Elite establishment, Fellow of the Royal Society and a prominent Freemason, so strongly not just encouraged, but forcefully asserted and promoted. He was also the grandfather of Aldous Huxley, author of '*Brave New World*', a dystopian novel written in the 1930s, and very similar to George Orwell's '*1984*', in that both novels depict a future society where the masses are suppressed and manipulated by mass propaganda, programmes of mind control and campaigns of lies. And another grandson of Thomas Henry Huxley was Julian Huxley - the very same Julian Huxley who became the first secretary-general of UNESCO, a branch of the Elite-controlled United Nations. Now there is no such thing as chance or coincidence, as I have explained in many of my previous books. There is just synchronicity, and whatever happens in the world of politics has already been planned! So please, - work this one out for yourself!

Canadian scientist, W.R Thomson writes:

'I am not satisfied that Darwin proved his point or that his influence in scientific and public thinking has been beneficial. The success of Darwinism was accompanied by a decline in scientific integrity.' ('*The Falsification of History*', John Hamer, page 48)

An opinion shared by Colin Patterson, senior palaeontologist at the London Museum of Natural History:

'In a way some aspects of Darwinism and of neo-Darwinism seem to me to have held back the progress of science.' ('*The Falsification of History*', John Hamer, page 48)

In their book, '*The Hidden History of the Human Race*' published in 1998, Michael Cremo and Richard Thompson convincingly show, -

with literally thousands of case studies and examples of mainstream archaeological cover-up operations, to prevent the truth becoming widely known, - how we have been duped into believing that homo-sapiens is much less than one million years old and is a product of evolution from apes. In the foreword to the book, written by Graham Hancock author of *'Fingerprints of the Gods',* Hancock writes:

'Cremo and Thomson's central proposition is that the model of human pre-history, carefully built-up by scholars over the past two centuries, is sadly and completely wrong. Moreover, the authors are not proposing that it can be put right with minor tinkering and adjustments. What is needed is for the existing model to be thrown out the window and for us to start again with open minds and with absolutely no preconceptions at all.

This is a position that is close to my own heart; indeed it forms the basis of my book 'Fingerprints of the Gods'. There, however, my focus was exclusively on the last 20,000 years and on the possibility that an advanced global civilization may have flourished more than 12,000 years ago only to be wiped out and forgotten in the great cataclysm that brought the last Ice Age to an end.

In 'The Hidden History of the Human Race' Cremo and Thompson go much further, pushing back the horizons of our amnesia not just 12,000 or 20,000 years, but millions of years into the past, and showing that almost everything we have been taught to believe about the origins and evolution of our species rests on the shaky foundation of academic opinion, and on a highly selective sampling of research results. The two authors then set about putting the record straight by showing all the other research results that have been edited out of the record during the past two centuries, not because there was anything wrong or bogus about the results themselves, but simply because they did not fit with prevailing academic opinion.........

In the final analysis, it is the meticulous scholarship of the authors, and the cumulative weight of the facts presented in 'The Hidden History of the Human Race' that really convince. The book is, I believe, in harmony with the mood of the public at large in the world today, a mood which no longer unquestioningly accepts the pronouncements of established authorities, and is willing to listen with an open mind...........Never before has the case for a complete re-evaluation of the human story been made more reasonably and rationally than it is in these pages.'

And the book to which Hancock is referring was published in 1998. Nearly 30 years ago now! And how humanity as a whole has moved on since then! How we have moved on simply as a result of the unearthing, the revealing, the exposing of scandal after scandal, scam after scam, corruption after corruption on the part of those who make the rules for the rest of us to obey!

And Cremo and Thompson point out the truth that there are many examples already found, and more continuing to be found, of human remains, some dating back several hundred million years! We have not been told the truth about the origins of humanity!

Despite it being just another **theory**, Darwinism has not been abandoned by the scientific community. But it has all been based on subjective interpretations, - posing, posturing, masquerading as facts!

That was then. But this is now. And we have moved on from the Earth-centered view of life. We now know that we humans and our little world are not the center of the entire universe. We now know that there are other, more intelligent forms of life and more advanced civilisations throughout the whole of the cosmos, many of whom have been in existence long before we materialised, and many of whom are as much as millions of light years ahead of us in technology and spiritual consciousness.

Unlike our modern-day cultures and civilisations, all ancient cultures linked humanity's origins to the heavens, and not to here on Planet Earth. The Egyptians, for example, were convinced in their belief that their ancestors came from the star Sirius and the star constellation of Orion, and they believed they themselves would return to be amongst the stars again. It is religion and science that today assert that life arose spontaneously here on this earth.

So, from where have we come? How did we get here? Where are we going?

And have we really descended from the apes?

Erich von Däniken in his book '*Evidence of the Gods*' answers this for us:

'The progression from ape to intelligent human is a farce with thousands of open questions and thousands of incomplete answers......

When I read that humans do not have fur because they learned to cover themselves with other furs, I feel that someone is pulling my leg. The pre-hominids are said to have descended from the trees for climatic reasons. What a thought! As if an ape species had realized that in evolutionary theory, it might be needed for humans at some point in the future! It climbed down from the trees but left its compatriots - don't they imitate everything?- swinging from branch to *branch in the trees to the present day. The social attitude of our ancestors left something to be desired.' (*Erich von Däniken, *'Evidence of the Gods',* page 190-191)

And what about natural selective evolution?

'I read, for example, that pre-hominids lived in packs and as a result developed intelligent and social behavior. Gruesome! Many animal species, not just apes, lived and live in packs. But apart from a hierarchy and pecking order, they have not developed any cultural intelligence.

*It is eternally argued that human beings are intelligent because they adapt better than other species. That objection is so much hot air. Why have other primates such as gorillas, chimpanzees, orangutans not 'adapted'? According to the rules of evolution, these cute animals would also have been 'compelled' to develop intelligence. You cannot apply evolution selectively to one chosen species............ Furthermore, there are much older life forms than the primates. Scorpions, cockroaches, or spiders, for example, have been shown to have existed more than 500 million years in the past. The same applies to various species of reptiles, some of which are even said to have descended from the dinosaurs. Now we know that crocodile mothers care lovingly for their young, but crocodile culture is nevertheless lacking, despite all the millions of years in which they have 'adapted'. Because they all survived so bravely, these species should have squirmed through much better than the incomparably younger Homo sapiens. Where are the art objects or burial sites of these creatures?' (*Erich von Däniken, *'Evidence of the Gods',* page 191)

Robert Bauval is one of the fore-runners in this field of investigation. He is the co-author of *'Cosmic Womb: The seeding of Planet Earth'* with **Chandra Wickramasinghe,** Ph.D., a professor of applied mathematics and astronomy and director of the Centre for Astrobiology at the University of Buckingham. In their book, the authors set out the theory of a cosmic origin for humanity, and ask, did the ancients know our true cosmic origins and have they left us clues? About '*Cosmic Womb',* Edward Steele, Ph.D., molecular immunologist writes:

'Beginning in the 1960s, Chandra Wickramasinghe, Ph.D., together with Fred Hoyle systematically founded the new science of astrobiology. Their discoveries and explanations - reported in numerous scientific papers and eloquently written books - put them in a class of their own, in the same pantheon of scientific immortals as Nicholas Copernicus, Galileo Galilei, Johannes Kepler, Isaac Newton, and Charles Darwin. And now, the brilliant astrophysicist and astrobiologist Chandra Wickramasinghe, Ph.D., has joined with Robert Bauval in bringing 'Cosmic Womb' to a new early 21st-century audience.'

And he asserts:

'Cosmic Womb is required reading for all those who want to understand the origins of life on Earth and throughout the cosmos. It is that important.'

And Chris H. Hardy, Ph.D., systems scientist and author of '*DNA of the Gods*', '*Wars of the Anunnaki*' and '*Cosmic DNA at the Origin*', writes:

'A fascinating book based on cutting-edge science that gives us twofold, compelling evidence - first that life (as molecules or basic bacteria) seeded in the whole cosmos via comets and hence there is a high probability of advanced intelligent civilizations all around us, and

second, the embedding of pi, phi, geodetic units, the circumference of Earth, and the speed of light in the Great Pyramid leaves us no alternative but to admit that such a highly scientific civilization has indeed left its imprint on our planet.'

In 1960 at Cambridge, Wickramasinghe, under the supervision of iconic astronomer and astrophysicist Sir Fred Hoyle, was exploring how life began here on earth. Hoyle himself had changed the way we think about the universe more than anyone had done for over a century, and by 1962 Hoyle and Wickramasinghe were convinced that interstellar dust provided the chemical fabric from which life must have originated, and he collaborated on the theory of *'panspermia'*, which postulates that life originated in the cosmos long before the formation of our solar system and that it was carried to earth by comets.

Bauval writes:

'Wickramasinghe learned from Hoyle that scientific opinions held by scientists, no matter how eminent they might be, should always be questioned. Hypotheses and theories are there to be continuously challenged and rigorously tested against the data that emerges from the real world. The history of science makes it amply clear that in all past ages authority stifled and strangled the progress to science. It is no different today. Blind adherence to authority must therefore be condemned.' (*Cosmic Womb'*, Introduction, page X)

The *'panspermia'* theory arises from the Swedish Nobel Prize winner Svante Arrhenius (1859-1927). And expanding on the panspermia theory developed with the celebrated astronomer Sir Fred Hoyle - namely that the building blocks of life were imported to Earth by comets in the distant past - Bauval and Wickramasinghe explore the latest findings in support of a cosmic origin for humanity. They detail the astrobiological discoveries of organic molecules deep in space, how molecules are incredibly resistant to the harshest conditions of space - enabling the transfer of genes from one star to another, and the recent recovery of microorganisms from comets still in space. They argue that the universe was *'born'* and preset with the blueprint of life and that the cosmos must be teeming with lifeforms far older and perhaps far more developed than us. They show how life arrived on our planet in the form of interstellar dust containing alien bacteria approximately 3.8 billion years ago and how later comets, meteoroids and asteroids brought new bacterial and viral genetic material that was vital for evolution.

So, what we are being told is that **humanity was seeded from space, but evolved on Earth.**

Using the latest advances in physics, cosmology, and neuroscience, Bauval and Wickramasinghe explore how universal knowledge may be stored in human DNA and cells, and they postulate that ancient cultures, such as the pyramid builders of Egypt and the temple builders of India, may have known a way to retrieve this knowledge. Sharing new discoveries from experienced architects, engineers, and mathematicians, they show how the Great Pyramid is a three-dimensional mathematical equation in stone, bearing a potent message for humanity across time and space about who we are and where we come from.

'In all past ages people have suffered from wrong ideas about the nature of the world often mistaking speculation for fact. The wrong ideas were often passionately defended until eventually with the arrival of new facts they came to be overturned and replaced. The idea

of an Earth-centered universe was the order of the day for the astronomer Omar Khayyam in eleventh-century Persia. Geocentric cosmology so placing Earth at the center of things prevailed throughout Europe from the time of the Rubayyat well into the Elizabethan era. The slow process of demoting the Earth from the center of things began at the beginning of the sixteenth century. The Copernican revolution, beginning with publication by Copernicus of 'De Revolutionibus Orbium Celestium' in 1543, progressing through the trial of Galileo Galilei, and culminating in the efforts of Tycho Brahe, Kepler, and Newton, finally removed the Earth from its privileged position of centrality in the solar system. This trend in which our place in the cosmos became diminished continued with advances in astronomy through the nineteenth, twentieth, and twenty-first centuries. Newer and more powerful telescopes and equipment combined with deployment of spacecraft continue to contribute to this process. We now know that our solar system is one of hundreds of billions of similar planetary systems in our Milky Way galaxy, which itself is one of countless billions of galaxies in the observable universe.' (Chandra Wickramasinghe, Ph.D. and Robert Bauval, *'Cosmic Womb: The Seeding of Planet Earth'* page 7-8)

And again, the most important point made in the book is:

'The material of all earthly life, including ourselves, is derived from atoms that owe their existence to cosmic processes. The carbon, oxygen, nitrogen, phosphorus, and metals in our bodies were all synthesized in the deep interiors of stars and were scattered into our midst by massive stars that exploded at the end of their lives - supernovae.' (Wickramasinghe and Bauval, *'Cosmic Womb'* page 8)

So Bauval and Wickramasinghe challenge us to accept the idea that the seed of life on Earth originated long ago in the cosmos, that it was carried to our planet by comets, and that an ET or advanced civilisation contact might have taken place in the past.

And what about the Big Bang? As Bauval and Wickramasinghe claim:

'It must be admitted that the standard big bang cosmology does indeed look very much like a modern rendering of the Judeo-Christian story of creation.'

'This is the so-called cosmological theory, elegantly crafted in mathematical formulation and widely supported by a vast and powerful scientific establishment. But for sure it is not cast in stone. It has to be admitted that a sizeable chunk of relevant ideas still occupy the realm of speculation, and societal and cultural constraints play a crucial role in defense of this model...........It seems likely that the currently favored big bang cosmology will require serious revision in the fullness of time. Modern astronomical data on galaxies forming some four hundred million years (a twinkling of an eye) after the big bang are beginning to strain the credibility of standard cosmologies.' ('*Cosmic Womb*' page 10)

'While evidence for life originating on Earth is fast vanishing, there still remains a mystery as to where the first self-replicable and evolvable living cell arose..............The possibility that the Earth was deliberately seeded with life designed by a superintelligent civilization thus remains a logical possibility. But that still begs the question of how and where the superintelligent civilization emerged. Perhaps we are witnessing a convergence of some abstract concept of God.' ('Cosmic Womb', page 17)

Otto Binder, to whom I have already referred in the previous chapter, is also an ardent advocate of the theory that we here on earth were seeded from other planets. Words and phrases such as '*space-spawned civilization*', '*star sires*' and '*earth colony*' are constantly used by him when talking about the origins of life on Planet Earth. Binder based much of his work on that of **Max Flindt,** co-author with him in '*We Are The Children Of The Stars*', in which Flindt and Binder take Darwin to task on what they call '*one damning exception*' to his theory of evolution, - *the 'creature called Man'*. Flindt and Binder claim that the theory that modern humans are hybrids of early humans and extra-terrestrial beings '*rings truer than ever before*'. In their evidence they reveal that Earth has been visited more than 5,000 times by creatures from other planets; that starmen deliberately hid any '*missing link*' human fossils in order to keep humankind from knowing it was a colony and they point out clues in the evolutionary record, along with hidden evidence in fossils, human reproduction and the advancement of our brains as showing us clearly that we have been colonised by other civilisations from space.

In '*We Are The Children Of The Stars*', Binder and Flindt explain the purpose of their book:

'*This book is concerned with the strong possibility - almost a probability, in our measured opinions - that mankind on Earth may have had superintelligent ancestors from outer space. Man may therefore be a hybrid, partly of terrestrial origin, partly extraterrestrial. There exists an incredible number of amazingly persuasive 'proofs' in support of this theory, which are duly presented in the pages ahead.*' ('*We Are The Children Of The Stars*', Introduction, page XV)

And in '*Ancient Aliens And Other Unsolved Mysteries Of The Past*', Binder points out:

'But it is in the Bible itself, in one very controversial passage over which theologians still wrangle today, that suggests the strongest evidence of hybridization between sky people and earth people.' (Otto Binder, *'Ancient Aliens'*, page 15)

And that very controversial passage?

'And the sons of God saw that the daughters of men were fair, and they took to wife such of them as they chose.' (Genesis 4:1)

But as Binder asks, who were these *'sons of God'*? And he maintains that the logical answer from the evidence we have, is that they were saucermen from space. And these *'godlike men who came from the sky'* according to legend, came to create man.

And as further evidence for their claims, that mankind is a half-earthly, half-starborn hybrid, deliberately created as a colony, Flindt and Binder point out the traits that are peculiar to this species alone, on earth:

'Shedding of tears; super-sensitive skin; lack of tooth-gaps; overweight brain; production of moronic genius; subject to schizophrenia; head hair; slow swallowing; lack of penis bone; oversized penis; production of genius; human infant's head much larger proportionately than newborn of animals; prevalence of Caesarian operations today a result of oversized infant from starmen heritage; long childhood of humans, exceeding animal weaning by far, indicating long-lived ancestry from starmen; imagination unique to human mind - no discernible signs in any animals; hybrid man not sterile, like mule, indicating mutant manipulation impossible to natural evolution; no new species of mammals for millions of years, except man; feelings of destiny and of religion in man; giants like Heidelberg and Java Man, always occur in

hybridization experiments in today's labs.' (Otto Binder, 'Ancient Aliens' page 147)

And from the great to the small:

'Going from the great to the small, were dwarfs as well as giants produced during the saucermen's experiments? The many legends of gnomes, goblins, kobolds, trolls, pixies, and other tiny people are too persistent and universal to be sheer invention. Then, our present day African pygmies are living proof that some branch of humanity turned small in the remote past- or were made to turn small by the saucermen. Pygmy fossils, though rare, have been found, dating back several hundreds of thousands of years.

Now, dwarfs or midgets show up quite regularly among normal humans today. This would indicate that the saucermen experimented with pygmy hybrid too, long ago, in an attempt to find the ideal colonist crossbreed. Small men might be more deft and nimble. And it is noticeable that dwarfs - whether living humans or fabled characters - have large heads in proportion to their small bodies. Thus, a dwarf's brain could still be the same size as that of a normal human.

A remarkable coincidence now arises. Most of the UFO landing reports of today, where the occupants step out, involve the well-known 'little men humanoids', averaging about three and a half feet tall.

What is the significance of the dwarf saucermen that are visiting us today?

One answer is that unlike earthlings, the saucermen on their world have deliberately bred themselves into different types - small humanoids, normal men, powerful giants, perhaps even the monster men reported at times at saucer landings in West Virginia and elsewhere. All of them would have a purpose to serve, in their complex society. The idea of uniformity in the human race as a necessary or desirable thing is simply one of our preconceived prejudices. We may someday, when we can manipulate the human form, also find it useful to try for variety in size and characteristics.' (Otto Binder, 'Ancient Aliens' page 22)

Binder and Flindt maintain:

'Earth is a colony or breeding ground originally established by outer-space peoples.' (Otto Binder, '*Ancient Aliens*' page 35)

And:

'.........present-day mankind was being fashioned out of biological crossbreeding experiments by outer-space colonizers.

We can suspect that some of the experiments turned out badly..........we can speculate even further that monsters were unwittingly produced in some of their bio-experiments.

Who knows but what the satyr with great hooves, the centaur or other mythological monstrosities were the results of misbreeding programs tried out by the spacemen in order to thoroughly understand the genetic complexities of earthly life-forms.' (Otto Binder, 'Ancient Aliens' page 20)

'It can be assumed that the saucermen were, and are, masters of biology far beyond the bio-arts known to us......whatever their unknown techniques, the saucermen had the ability to mold, change, and modify their earth hybrids and condense evolutionary processes into brief periods of time - exactly the same way modern genetics grow

generations of fruit flies and guide them into wholesale evolutionary changes.' (Otto Binder, *'Ancient Aliens'* page 21)

'The universe is crammed with earthlike worlds which spawned a thinking animal quite like man, either indigenously or through programs of interbreeding.' (Otto Binder, *'Ancient Aliens'* page 111)

'But undeniably, Mr. Flindt has gone a long step in proving that the riddle of mankind being a misfit in evolution does have an answer.' (Otto Binder, *'Ancient* Aliens' page 148)

And that answer? **It's in the stars**!

Max Flindt, 1915-1974, dedicated his life to independent scientific research, working at numerous prestigious laboratories, including Lockheed where he was engaged in highly classified space research. He was the first person to ever scientifically document from biological evidence the possibility that humankind may be a hybrid of terrestrial humanoids and starmen.

Flindt supports his hypothesis by pointing out that man's brain is more than triple the weight of other animals; that man alone out of hundreds of rival mammalian species, developed this tremendous brain power; that man, uniquely, possesses almost no body hair and that man alone, unlike all the other animals in nature, comes in a variety of skin colours, statures, cranial shapes, colour of head hair, and facial features. Flint argues that none of these facts can be explained by the theory of evolution. He furthermore points out that *'apes and chimpanzees never come up with geniuses',* nor are there any genius horses or dogs:

'Only the introduction of extraneous super-intellect genes into the

mainstream of human life, long ago, could account for a Ptolemy, Galileo, Newton, Edison, Einstein, and all the other great brains that have appeared throughout history.

And only great-brained men from extraterrestrial sources could have injected those super-genes into the racial bloodstream of mankind on earth. Otherwise, science and biology simply have no explanation for genius except to call it a fortunate mixture of genes and chromosomes - a process that does not happen with other animals and which is therefore highly suspect. It goes against nature, as defined by science.' (Otto Binder, *'Ancient Aliens'* page 19)

And what about those giant people we read about in various texts? Those giant people who are believed to have inhabited our earth at one time?

"The Bible, again, gives us a brain-teaser that has its roots in some extraordinary biological event in pre-history. 'There were giants in the earth in those days; and also after that, when the sons of God came in unto the daughters of men, and bear children unto them, the same mighty men which were of old, men of renown.' (Genesis 6: 2, 4)

'Men of renown' would seem to mean genius, but 'mighty men' refers apparently to superb physical specimens. Remember that all primates and primitive sub-humans were creatures of short stature, never as tall as modern men. The matings with tall starmen would result in giants physically and men of renown mentally." (Otto Binder, *'Ancient Aliens'* page 19)

So, according to Binder and Flindt, we are a product of **'Space Bio-Inheritance'**, each of us a *'hybrid from the union of ancient spacemen and some earthly species of man-ape who existed, according to recent* *anthropological finds, as long as two million years ago.'*

Will Hart is a writer and photojournalist who has been investigating UFOs and history's mysteries since 1968. He has appeared on the TV show '*Ancient Aliens*' and his work has featured in '*Atlantis Rising, 'New Dawn', 'UFO', 'Nexus', 'Wild West', 'Sierra Heritage',* and '*Nature Photography'*. He is the author of several books, including '*The Genesis Race*' and '*Ancient Alien Ancestors: Advanced Technologies That Terraformed Our World'*. In his book '*Ancient Alien Ancestors*' Hart explains that in the early 1970s, Nobel Prize-winning DNA codiscoverer Sir Francis Crick and his colleague Leslie Orgel proposed that in the distant past, an extraterrestrial race sent a spacecraft loaded with microorganisms to seed Earth with life. Now, more than 40 years later, the fields of space research and biotechnology have advanced to the point where they can back up Crick and Orgel's claims about our ancient alien ancestors.

'The notion that life originated elsewhere in the universe and later arrived on Earth is not the stuff of any science fiction writer's imagination. Today it is a solid scientific theory that explains how life came to Earth from the cosmos.

*The first documented mention of the idea appears in the writings of the fifth-century BCE Greek philosopher Anaxagoras. He called his thesis 'Panspermia', a Greek term that means 'seeds everywhere'. (*Will Hart, *'Ancient Alien Ancestors'* page 6)

Will Hart, like the other writers we have so far looked at explains:

'Artifacts, sacred texts, and oral traditions from human history tell of 'gods' descending from outer space to Earth. These alien 'gods', the Genesis Race, had as their mission to seed life on the planet and to

extend their civilization through the creation of humankind.' ('Ancient Alien Ancestors' page 1)

And the purpose of his book:

'I present the scientific basis for the theory of 'directed panspermia', which posits that life, via microorganism, was shipped to Earth by extraterrestrial civilization.'

And he makes clear:

'The concept of 'The Genesis Race' is a theoretical framework that goes beyond the general theory and shows that there is extensive ancient and modern-day evidence of extraterrestrial involvement, contact, and colonization of the earth.'

'Directed panspermia is simply the idea that the seeds of life originated elsewhere and were deliberately shipped to earth from an extraterrestrial planet long ago. To that basic concept, I have added the evidence in support of the notion that these same extraterrestrials actually set foot on earth and intervened in human history. Cosmic ancestry and extraterrestrial visitation are not new phenomena that exist outside the bounds of science.' (Will Hart, 'Ancient Alien Ancestors' page 2)

'Directed panspermia, via the Genesis Race, only requires that one civilization in the entire universe triumphed over every obstacle and has been able to travel the vast expanses of space to transmit life to other worlds.' (Will Hart, 'Ancient Alien Ancestors' page 2-3)

Hart shows how the Earth was terraformed through an engineering programme, so sophisticated and vast that it has escaped our attention so far - for example, the major rivers on Earth are precisely aligned through geo-engineering with the Great Pyramid of Giza. Revealing the Great Pyramid as an alien message in stone, Hart explains how the Giza pyramids could not have been built by the ancient Egyptians and examines the extraterrestrial energy technologies used to move the massive stone blocks, methods later rediscovered by Nikola Tesla, and the builder of Coral Castle, Edward Leedskalnin. He details how an advanced race implanted the basic genome on Earth as well as genetically engineered the human race, and shows how our spectrum of blood types supports the theory of panspermia while directly contradicting the conventional '*out of Africa*' theory of evolution.

And furthermore, Hart investigates how the extraterrestrial agency behind the origin of civilisation is still working behind the scenes today. He argues that the strongest UFO sightings point to an advanced ET civilisation that is not an alien race in the way we normally think of '*aliens*', - they are our ancestors and as human as we are.

Ellis Silver Ph.D., a leading environmentalist and ecologist, in his book '*Humans are not from* Earth', also supports these theories. His book is an evaluation of the evidence for, but mostly against, man's evolution on Planet Earth. He includes 53 reasons why we could not have evolved on Earth, including, for example: the sun dazzles us, and damages our eyes and skin; the varying degree of thickness of our skin; our lack of hair; our low vitamin D levels; we wear clothes; our chronic illnesses and medical conditions; we eat meat, but we shouldn't; we dislike natural foods; we have food cravings; we survive, but we don't thrive; we can't sense natural disasters; our poor sense of direction; our reaction to carbon dioxide; birth issues and our destruction of our resources and environment.

Put simply, our bodies are so poorly adapted to living on this Earth that it is obvious we did not evolve here. In comparison, Earth's native creatures are well adapted.

Silver answers the questions: where is our real home planet and what is it like? Why are we here on Earth? When and how did we arrive? What about God, religion, DNA and evolution? What do we really know about extraterrestrials? Why is valid evidence covered up, denied and ignored?

Silver writes:

'We are hybrids of ancient hominins and aliens'

and:

'My own hypothesis is that we started out as natural hominins that evolved on our home planet, not on Earth. The first groups of us that were brought to Earth were 'pure' unmodified humans. But we didn't survive for very long.

So the aliens began tweaking our genomes to address the problem. Some of the DNA they used probably came from the more robust Earth hominins. It would have made sense to use them, as they were already here, it would have been easy to harvest DNA from them, and they could obviously survive the conditions of that time.

That didn't work either though - we still weren't able to survive here. So over the next few hundred years, then tweaked our genomes so more, using DNA from themselves and other alien species. Eventually, as we all know, they succeeded.

And that makes us a complex mixture of pure humans from our home planet, with parts of at least one alien species, (and probably several more), plus parts of at least one hominin species from Earth.' (Ellis Silver, *'Humans are not from Earth'* page 274)

So where on Planet Earth were we *'dropped off'*?

According to Silver:

'There's evidence that the first of these groups were dropped off in Israel, Spain and Australia. The next group were probably dropped off in Central or Southern America, India and China. Around 300,000 years ago, the African groups arrived. One was dropped in North Africa, specifically present-day Morocco. The other, which was by far the largest of all the groups, was dropped in East Africa, present-day Ethiopia, Kenya, Somalia, Eritrea and Djibouti.' (*'Humans are not from Earth'*, page 196)

And as well as the *'directed panspermia'* theory, Silver also posits the *'reverse panspermia'* theory, which suggests that other planets may have been seeded with life from Earth. For example, the asteroid that is suspected to have hit the Earth 66 million years ago, resulting in the extinction of the dinosaurs, could have blasted millions of individual rocks into space. Some of them may have landed on other planets and moons in our own solar system, and a few could have reached planets around other stars.

And from where have we come? Where is our home planet?

'We couldn't have evolved from any hominin on Earth, but we did evolve from a hominin on our home planet. Our home planet is considerably older than the Earth, and its various civilizations would have been (and might still be) more advanced than ours. Evolution

proceeded on our home planet in much the same way as it did here.' (Ellis Silver, *'Humans are not from Earth'* page 389)

And why are we here?

'Perhaps we were removed from our natural environment because of the problems we were causing: violence, destruction, over-consumption of resources, driving other species to extinction and so on........

Perhaps we were brought here as a natural predator to help cull a species that was getting out of control........

I doubt the aliens ever envisaged we would take over the planet to the extent we have. Unfortunately, the time could be drawing close when they decide that we also need culling. They could do this simply by introducing a virus that we have no immunity to. In fact, they might have already tried this several times: hence the numerous plagues, and viruses such as AIDS and SARS that apparently sprang out of nowhere. We survived those - as a species at least - but there could be worse to come if they decide to try again.' (Ellis Silver, *'Human are not from Earth'* page 428)

What did we just read? -

'There could be worse to come if they decide to try again.'

Silver's book was published in 2017. And we all know what arrived *'unexpectedly'*, just a few short years later! And one is almost tempted to say *'out of nowhere'* - but that is not actually the case! What happened was neither unforeseen nor any sort of accident or chance happening. That's not the way politics works! Anything, no matter what, that happens in politics, is always planned! Always part of an agenda! And our world changed forever!

Jason Quitt, co-author with Bob Mitchell of '*Forbidden Knowledge: Revelations of a multi-dimensional time traveler*' has revealed his own personal experiences as a multi-dimensional traveler. He has experienced the past, the present and the future, from ancient Egypt and Atlantis to our possible future. He has been a witness to our un-recorded history. Quitt explains how our world is not what we think it is, but a world once fought and protected by other-worldly and dimensional beings. An ascension process is under way right now that is awakening our consciousness to look beyond the veils of our known reality. We are once again remembering our place in the universe as multi-dimensional, inter-galactic beings who are having a temporary physical experience here on Planet Earth. Quitt writes:

'The Pleiades is a star cluster in the constellation Taurus and among the nearest star clusters to Earth located about 500 light years from our planet. There is evidence this star cluster was known to virtually all of the ancient cultures, including the Mayans, the Aztecs, ancient Chinese and Japanese, Native American and Canadians and of course, the ancient Egyptians. According to ancient alien theorists and some UFOlogists, the star system is also the home of an extraterrestrial species known as the Pleiadians.' (Jason Quitt, '*Forbidden Knowledge*' page 66)

So, are we descendants of the Pleiadians?

And Quitt agrees with the ancient alien theory that mankind wasn't the product of natural evolution, but was created as a result of the genetic manipulation of the then native Earth hominids with DNA of extraterrestrial origins.

And what about Darwin and his theory of selective evolution?

Back again to Binder and Flindt, and the purpose of their book '*We are the Children of the Stars*':

'This book is concerned with the strong possibility - almost a probability, in our most measured opinions - that mankind on Earth may have had superintelligent ancestors from outer space. Man may therefore be a hybrid, partly of terrestrial origin, partly extraterrestrial. There exist an incredible number of amazingly persuasive 'proofs' in support of this theory......

Those proofs or evidence of the theory's validity will be found virtually everywhere around us - in our bodies, our brains and minds, our histories, our archeological and anthropological pursuits, and in many other unexpected areas of the humanities and sciences.

This book might very well be titled 'On Tiptoe Beyond Darwin', for we have in reality 'extended' Evolution beyond the limited scope of natural selection on Earth, to an expanded concept that might be called 'Astro Evolution', or Evolution from the Stars.

We wish to state at the outset, however, that we do not condemn or recommend casting aside the great Theory of Evolution. We believe, along with any biologist or scientist, that its basic premise apparently explains the whole programme of life on Earth, from its earliest beginnings in primeval times to the amazing proliferation of creatures today - with one notable exception. That exception, that one damning exception, is the creature called Man.

He alone, of all species, plagues the Theory of Evolution and, in fact, shakes its foundations. For by no stretch of available facts (or even imagination) can human beings be products solely of orthodox Evolution and its classic rules.

Yet, we reiterate that Darwin's theory seems to cover adequately all other animate life on Earth. It only fails, and fails dismally, in explaining you and me.' (Binder and Flint, *'We are the Children of the Stars'* page xv-xvi)

And quoting from Norman MacBeth's *'Darwin Retried'*:

'Darwin was an amateur. He did not teach in a university or work in a laboratory. He 'did' science in his own house with no trained staff and very little (fossil) equipment.'

Norman Macbeth was a Harvard-trained lawyer by profession, and while recovering from a long illness, he began a study of Darwinism evolution. He finished his first major book on the subject with the thought, *'If I had to oppose that man in court I could get his case thrown out.'*

In *'Darwin Retried',* Macbeth exposes gaps in the evidence and errors in the reasoning behind Darwinism. He suggests that a fresh start is in order and, in the present state of affairs, no theory at all may be preferable to the existing one.

Macbeth writes:

'If I were attacking Darwin's character, as Samuel Butler did, it would only be natural for his admirers to rush to his defense. If I were impugning his intelligence, as Barzun sometimes does, again it would be natural for them to protest. But I am asserting only that he is not the last word in science and that his theory has not been proved adequate.' (*'Darwin Retried'*, Norman Macbeth, page 149)

Binder and Flint continue:

'Thus we see that all later adherents of Evolution most of them very eminent scientists, were in truth only following the theory of an amateur, an unskilled (in academic terms) nonprofessional with an 'untrained' mind in comparison with the later experts and authorities who took up his tremendous basic idea with the fervor of zealots.

We are amateurs and Darwin was an amateur.

*That, in a sense, 'equates' us as having the same full right as nonprofessional Darwin to exercise our studied viewpoints on Evolution. And to present - as **Darwinlike amateurs,** if you wish - a wholly new theory as to the origin of Man.' (*Binder and Flint, 'We are the Children of the Stars' page xvi-xvii)

And that alternative to Darwin's theory? In Binder and Flint's book, that alternative is the concept of **Hybrid Man** and the **Earth Colony.** An alternative concept based on the observation and belief that Mankind is an *'anomaly'*, a maddening *'misfit'*, in the *'grand sweep of survival of the fittest. His physiological body might have evolved from lower forms of animals, but his amazing brain, - never.'*

Binder and Flint concentrate on various shortcomings of Darwin's theory in explaining Man, - the *'misfit'* of Evolution:

1. The **explosive** beginnings of life on Earth, 500 million to 600 million years ago.

2. Why is it that an analysis of the six spreading movements of primitive Man indicates that three of these spreading movements have come from Asia Minor?

3. Unexplained greater size of brain of prehistoric Man, compared to Modern Man.

4. Lack of explanation for Man's greater intelligence arising out of strict evolution.

5. Lack of explanation for Man's greater brain weight compared to other animals.

6. Why is it that Man is unique in so many ways among all primates that roam the world?

7. The tool riddle: Why were shaped tools invented and used solely by all species of early ape-men - Hominids - but not by any other animals?

8. The civilisation mystery: Why did the homo branches of both Neanderthal Man and Cro-Magnon, who had brain-cases larger than modern Man, never, through a period of 60,000 years, create civilisation, living instead as brutes?

9. The intelligence enigma: Why did civilisation spring up with an abruptness, in Sumeria, circa 10,000 BC? How could mankind change from a neolithic savage who was a nomadic hunter to a social being with villages and agriculture? Overnight, so to speak? What can explain the skilled map-making art prior to Columbus, exemplified by the astonishing Piri Reis map that shows accurate detail of South America and of Antarctica? Of Antarctica before the last Ice Age some 10,000 years ago? Where did the ancients, as long as 2,000 years ago, learn an advanced form of mathematics that allowed calculations of the Earth's size, and pinpoint the eclipses of the sun and moon?

10. Mental phenomena in Man: Why is it that no ape brain, according

to exhaustive tests, displays the fantastic higher qualities of Man's brain, such as genius, imagination, scientific inspiration, and less flatteringly, schizophrenia?

11. The thinking puzzle: Why do human beings alone, apart from any animal, have religion? The exploratory instinct sparked by curiosity alone? The sense of high destiny? The feeling that life has a meaning?

12. Mythological enigma: Why does the mythology of **every one of Earth's cultures** in the past tell the same general tale, that the human race either came from the stars, or that **'gods'** visited Earth and helped us launch civilisation?

In their investigation into strong evidence for all of this and their explanation for it all, Binder and Flindt lead us to the viable conclusion that man may indeed be a star-crossed hybrid of two worlds and furthermore, that mankind is indeed a colony of the starmen by conscious design or plan that is still being withheld from us Earth people.

All just too unbelievable? Too incredible? Too difficult to accept?

But remember! All great truths begin as being considered ridiculous and totally unacceptable!

Darwin's revolutionary *'Theory of Evolution'*, published in 1858 did indeed become universally accepted worldwide. But! As Binder and Flint point out, it has failed to establish itself firmly without question.

And why? Obviously because since then, many new discoveries have been made in every field of science, and also obviously because since then, so many untruths have all been exposed!

So! Is it now time for a new theory to replace that of Darwin? Outdated and no longer acceptable as it is?

Has Darwin become redundant? Time up for Darwin? Time for Darwin to move over?

Time for us to accept that we, humanity, are the exception to the rule of natural selection applicable to all other animals? Time for us to see the anomaly that we are? Time for us to accept that we are the contrary exception to the classic workings of the laws of evolution? Time for us to accept that we are **Hybrid Man**, and a **colony** of some other species in the Cosmos?

And time for us to accept that we, intelligent man, are a product of genetic engineering? Genetic engineering by other-worldly beings, known to us as extraterrestrials, advanced civilisations out there somewhere in the Cosmos, with technology so far in advance of us that we cannot even imagine what it might be?

So what exactly do these ancient Sumerian and Babylonian texts tell us?

Before we look, we need to first consider Mesopotamia, Sumeria and Babylon as the *'cradle of civilisation'*.

Chapter 4:

The 'Cradle of Civilisation' - Mesopotamia, Sumeria, Babylon

Cast your mind to the geographical area of our world that we now know as modern-day Iraq. Yes, we tend to see Iraq now as a war-torn country, refugees flooding out to find better lives elsewhere in our decimated world. But it was not always like that!

Now allow your imagination to conjure up images of the exotic, the mysterious, the mythical, the mystical, with names such as Baghdad, the Hanging Gardens of Babylon, Nineveh, - all exotic, mysterious places, and all far removed from us in time and place. Black, starry Arabian night skies, not forgetting Aladdin's Cave and Aladdin and the Magic Carpet! And the names of those earliest, first cities, - names such as Eridu, Uruk, Ur and Lagash.

And of course, the *'Rose City'*, Petra, or the *'Petrified City',* an ancient city and centre of an Arab kingdom in Hellenistic and Roman times, the ruins of which are in southwest Jordan. A honeycomb of hand-hewn caves, temples, and tombs carved from blushing pink sandstone in the high desert of Jordan some 2,000 years ago. Hidden by time and shifting sand, Petra tells of a lost civilisation. Little is known about the Nabateans, - a nomadic desert people whose kingdom rose up from these cliffs and peaks, and whose incredible wealth grew from the lucrative incense trade.

All part of an ancient civilisation! - The ancient civilisation of Mesopotamia!

There is no universally accepted timeline for settlements in ancient Mesopotamia, but it is generally agreed by scholars that semi-nomadic hunter-gatherers had been settling there from around 10,000 to 8,000 BCE. Signs were found of cultivated date palms even before 10,000 BCE in the south, where Sumer would later be founded. The Sumerian people arriving in southern Mesopotamia called themselves the '*black-headed people*', joining other nomadic and semi-nomadic peoples settling between the Euphrates and Tigris Rivers and throughout the ancient Near East. It was these Sumerians who invented writing and later recorded the history, myths, and beliefs of earlier generations from oral transmissions.

Mesopotamia! That ancient civilisation that gave us not only the wheel, hydraulic irrigation and agricultural implements, but an enormous list of other creations over their extraordinarily long period of dominance in writing, construction, science, law, literature, poetry, music, and the building of great empires. That ancient civilisation that laid the foundations and framework for us in today's world. That ancient civilisation whose first cities emerged in the fifth millennium BCE, with Eridu, the city of the '*god*' Enki, being founded sometime around the year 5,000 BCE, followed around 500 years later by the city of Uruk, ruled by the '*goddess*' Inanna, daughter of Enki. An ancient civilisation made up of several major empires, numerous cities, spread across an extended period of history, and inclusive of hundreds of different ethnic groups of people, - a mixed pot, a simmering, brewing cauldron!

But nothing lasts forever! - No great empire, state or civilisation is permanent! And it is the most controlled, ideological states that last for only a very short period of time! History is permeated with the meteoric rise and the subsequent fall of great empires, great states, great civilisations. The ebb and flow! The rise and fall of great civilisations! The swing of the pendulum! Where now is the glory that was Egypt? Where now is the glory that was Greece? Where now is the glory that was Rome? And Mesopotamia? - For Mesopotamia, the decline was equally inevitable.

So first of all, where are these places? - Mesopotamia, Babylon, Sumeria.

In a far-off time, across Europe and Asia there were four of what we call the '*cradles of civilisation*', Egypt, China, India and Mesopotamia, - each one of them built along a great river. The great civilisation of Egypt rose along the banks of the River Nile, and dominated the Mediterranean area for over several thousand years BCE, until Alexander the Great, a king of the ancient Greek kingdom of Macedon, 336-323 BCE, secured dominance; the earliest Chinese civilisation rose along the banks of the Yellow River, and the Indus Valley civilisation rose along the banks of the Indus River, in what is now modern-day Pakistan. But perhaps the most significant of all ancient civilisations was that of the Mesopotamians, a civilisation that rose in the fertile lands between the Rivers Euphrates and Tigris, where great empires rose and fell, in what is now modern-day Iraq and parts of Syria, Iran and Turkey. Ancient Sumer was in the southern part of Mesopotamia. Cities were built along the rivers Tigris and Euphrates. Being close to the rivers allowed people to grow crops, travel and transport goods easily. Mesopotamian civilisation was famous for its cities, - Ur, Uruk, Eridu, and Larsa being some of the largest.

And it is this great ancient Mesopotamian civilisation that is of paramount interest and significance for this book. The ancient Mesopotamian civilisation that was associated with Sumerians,

Persians, Assyrians, Akkadians and Babylonians.

The name '*Mesopotamia*' itself is a combination of the ancient term '*meso*', meaning between, and the word '*potamos*' meaning river, so '*Mesopotamia*' literally translates to '*between two rivers*'. Mesopotamia is known to be the first place where the progress of humanity began, developing from hunter-gatherer societies to an agricultural village community due to the rich fertile soil of the Tigris-Euphrates valley, and then through the urban revolution and into a more modern city-dwelling culture.

So what was the story of Creation according to these peoples of the ancient Mesopotamian civilisations?

Let us look at what they left us, - carved on their clay tablets!

And let us consider, are we reading myths and stories, - myths and stories being part of every culture and civilisation, - or are we reading history, an account of what actually happened?

Who knows?

Chapter 5:

Creation according to the ancient Sumerian Cuneiform Clay Tablets

Amongst the numerous *'firsts'* that the ancient Mesopotamians developed and passed down to us was the skill of writing. And their form of writing was the Cuneiform Clay Tablets.

Cuneiform is a style of writing where symbols and letters are etched into stone or clay so that their message can be preserved long into the future. Unlike paper, which has a relatively short lifespan, these cuneiform tablets can withstand fire and even devastating floods, which is the only reason they are still here today. The information and the stories they contain are key evidence to a past, knowledge about which is coming increasingly to light as new discoveries are unearthed, and disseminated and spread worldwide through the internet. Scholars continue to update the translations of the cuneiform tablets from all of these ancient civilisations that have a specific and very detailed history.

The bulk of our current knowledge stems from the excavated ancient library of King Ashurbanipal of Assyria in Nineveh. Ashurbanipal was the last of the Assyrian kings, and it was in 600 BCE that he formed the library with a clay tablet collection containing the literature of ancient Assyria, Sumer and Babylonia. More than 30,000 cuneiform clay tablets were discovered here, many in several languages and styles and many still to be deciphered. We are only at the beginning! Merely scratching the surface!

Prior to the 19th century, the bible was considered the oldest book in the world and its narratives were thought to be completely original. In the mid-19th century, however, European museums, as well as academic and religious institutions, sponsored excavations in Mesopotamia to find physical evidence for historical corroboration of the stories in the bible. These excavations found quite the opposite, however, in that, once cuneiform was translated, it was understood that a number of biblical narratives were actually Mesopotamian in origin.

Famous stories such as the Fall of Man and the Great Flood were originally conceived and written down in Sumer, translated and modified later in Babylon, and reworded by the Assyrians before they were used by the Hebrew scribes for the versions which later appeared in the bible.

And with the continuing dissemination of these translations come strong, seismic shock waves!

We are all familiar with the story of the creation of the first humans, as related in the Book of Genesis of the Christian Bible. Indeed we have been metaphorically *'bred and buttered'* on the story of Adam and Eve in the Garden of Eden. And of course, - not forgetting that serpent! And in my previous book *'The Soul Net!'* I dealt with the Gnostic story of creation, - Sophia, the Demiurge and the Archons.

And now here in the ancient Mesopotamian cuneiform clay tablets we have Anu, Enki, Enlil, Ninhursag and Marduk. All, - according to the ancient texts, - playing a significant role in the creation of humanity! So who were these beings? Did they actually exist? Or are they all shrouded in mythology?

It was in 1975 that the late Zachariah Sitchin (1920-2010) first shocked the world by his translation of these ancient scriptures, whereby he proposed that the god of the bible is actually taken from the Sumerian scriptures and is not one entity, but two, - two half-brothers, Enki and Enlil, sons of Anu, the '*god*' of the planet Nibiru, - which Sitchin claimed was a hitherto undiscovered planet, beyond Neptune, from where these beings hailed. His writings state that Nibiru approaches Earth once every 3,600 years and then retreats again to the depths of space.

Sitchin, an eminent Orientalist and biblical scholar, was distinguished by his ability to read these ancient writings of Mesopotamia and Persia mainly on their clay tablets and other ancient texts. He was born into a Jewish family in Baku, the capital of then Soviet Azerbaijan, and raised in Mandatory Palestine which in 1948 became the modern state of Israel. A graduate of the University of London, he worked as a journalist and editor in Israel for many years. He became convinced that Homo Sapiens are not the product of natural selection — at least, not entirely. According to his interpretations of ancient Mesopotamian texts and inscriptions, interpretations which have often been questioned and disputed, the first humans were bioengineered by some extraterrestrials called the Anunnaki, who once colonised southeastern Africa.

Indeed all of Sitchin's books, including '*The 12th Planet*', - the planet he named Nibiru, - and his follow-up books have been disputed and questioned by scientists and historians, but they have sold millions of copies nevertheless and have been translated into more than 25 languages. Similar to other authors such as Immanuel Velikovsky, Erich von Däniken, Robert Monroe and William Bramley, Sitchin advocated hypotheses in which extraterrestrial events supposedly played a significant role in ancient human history.

Wikipedia has just updated Sitchin's translations because there has been so much further research on them and we have so much more detailed information now. A lot of those texts that Sitchin could not get his hands on were private collections, now in the public domain, and this is where a lot of the new details come from. They are just some of hundreds and thousands of clay tablets found in what was Mesopotamia.

Sitchin's works have been questioned by many. And rightly so! Everything needs to be questioned!

But, and as is always the case, there are those who uphold and support Sitchin's work, including M. J. Evans, PH.D. Evans, longtime friend and colleague of Sitchin, accompanied Sitchin on several of his tours to ancient sites in the Mediterranean region, Europe and Mexico, and has appeared on TV *'Ancient Aliens'* to discuss his work.

In her book *'Zecharia Sitchin and the Extraterrestrial Origins of Humanity',* Evans writes in defense of Sitchin:

'Recently even more attacks against the validity of Sitchin's work and accuracy of his word translations have appeared on the Internet. The Internet can be used to facilitate the promulgation of ungrounded negative views as well as legitimate criticism. Sitchin was one of two hundred scholars (in the world) who could read and translate the Sumerian language in the late 1970s, and who worked with the ancient tablets. In doing his translations, he made use of his knowledge of Sumerian, Akkadian, Babylonian, and his understanding of Egyptian hieroglyphics. He also drew on his knowledge of ancient (as well as modern) Hebrew in order to work out specific word

meanings. One has to wonder if the linguistic critics are as broadly competent. Did they study the ancient tablets? Or did they use only the early translations and their interpretations that were written before the space age gave a key to the embedded messages?

Sadly, it is unlikely that any of Sitchin's critics have read the full body of his work, looked into the quality of his sources, and observed how he selectively used previously published material to document his findings. We doubt those critical voices have followed his logic with their own careful reading of not only Sitchin's original work, but also the sources he used. Putting any of these verification techniques into motion likely would put to rest any critical assaults. If the linguistic criticisms that have come forward are posed by someone who reads Sumerian, has studied Akkadian and Babylonian, has translated Egyptian hieroglyphics, has worked in ancient and modern Hebrew, and who speaks German as well as Hebrew, and who reads French, and of course works competently in English, then such a critic is qualified to launch criticism of Sitchin's linguistic interpretations.

One thing is for certain. Those who have identified themselves as negative Sitchin critics will find themselves on the wrong side of history as time moves forward and Sitchin's work is proved to be more and more accurate. Technological advances already have brought to light information that supports his findings...........

Zachariah Sitchin's work shakes up contemporary knowledge of science and cultural history.........' (M.J. Evans, *'Zechariah Sitchin and the Extraterrestrial Origins of Humanity'* page 19-20)

In her book, Evans draws upon her many conversations with Sitchin and provides an indepth analysis of his revelations about the Anunnaki, those extra-terrestrial beings who *'from heaven to Earth came'*, focusing on their activities on Earth and indeed on Earth's future. She explores the genesis of Sitchin's interest in the Nefilim, the leaders of the Anunnaki, and the controversy caused by the publication of Sitchin's first book *'The 12th Planet'*. She examines Sitchin's research into the Nefilim family tree, the Anunnaki arrival on Earth to mine gold to repair the atmosphere on their home planet, Nibiru, and their creation of modern humans as workers for their mines and to build their civilisation on Earth. She shows how, in the context of 21st century technological capabilities, Sitchin's work casts a different light on ancient events, with implications for our future. The author reveals the details of the love and lust proclivities of the Nefilim *'gods'* Anu, Enlil, Enki and the *'goddess'* Inanna/Ishtar and shows how we inherited these tendencies from our Anunnaki creators as well as their use of war for problem solving. Concluding with an examination of Sitchin's prediction of a nuclear war event on Earth in 2024 AD, she shows how we would be repeating the same aggressive warlike behaviors of our Anunnaki creators, who, she maintains, may very well become our saviors when Nibiru next returns to our solar system.

So according to Sitchin and Evans and others writing in support of Sitchin, Nibiru was the home planet of an advanced extraterrestrial race called the Anunnaki in Sumerian writings, whom Sitchin states are called the Nefilim in Genesis. He wrote that they evolved after Nibiru entered the inner Solar System, and they first arrived on Earth probably 450,000 years ago, looking for minerals, especially gold, which they found and mined in Africa. Sitchin states that these *'gods'* were the rank-and-file workers of the colonial expedition to Earth from the planet Nibiru.

And Enki, - the Sumerian *'god'* of water and human culture, -

suggested that to relieve the Anunnaki, who had mutinied over their dissatisfaction with their working conditions, that primitive workers, - Homo Sapiens, - be created by genetic engineering as slaves to replace them in the gold mines by crossing extraterrestrial genes with those of Homo Erectus. According to Sitchin, ancient inscriptions report that the human civilisation in Sumer, Mesopotamia, was set up under the guidance of these *'gods',* and human kingship was inaugurated to provide intermediaries between mankind and the Anunnaki, - creating the *'divine right of kings'* doctrine. Sitchin believed that fallout from nuclear weapons, used during a war between factions of the extraterrestrials, is the *'evil wind'* described in the *'Lament for Ur'* that destroyed the city of Ur around 2000 BC. Sitchin states the exact year is 2024 BCE. He claimed that his research coincides with many biblical texts, and that biblical texts come originally from Sumerian writings.

While many see these ancient writings as myth and story, Sitchin was convinced that they are historical documents. To him, the word *'Nefilim'* in the biblical Book of Genesis, actually means, not *'giants'* as in Genesis, but *'those who came down'*. And *'those who came down'* were, in Sitchin's belief, the ancient space travellers as told on the ancient Sumerian clay tablets. The earlier pioneering researchers and scholars before Sitchin had absolutely no concept of space travel, and so they believed the tablets were mythology. Sitchin, on the other hand, was conversant with space age technology and could recognise it in the ancient records. His own mastering of cosmology, celestial mechanics, and even genetic science, led him to his deep and profound belief that the ancient Sumerian clay tablets were historical records of what had actually happened so many thousands of years ago, - interplanetary travel by an ancient civilisation. An ancient civilisation, that like so many other ancient civilisations, was so far advanced from us, - some as many as millions of light years ahead of us, - that we cannot even begin to imagine their powers or their technology. An ancient civilisation that was able to come to Earth in their highly advanced space vehicles in order to mine the gold that was needed for their own home planet, to safeguard them against radiation. Gold! That most precious of metals! And still today, our modern astronauts wear gold-plated helmets and other gold-plated apparatus to protect them against excessive radiation. - No argument there!

Those *'gods'* from the sky who are prevalent throughout the bible! Indeed, it could be said that the bible is all about ETs! Called *'gods'* because, to those ancient people who witnessed them and drew and painted them on their cave walls and stone surfaces, they must have appeared as *'gods'*, coming down from the heavens. But were they simply *'extraterrestrials'*, whose orbiting planet was in close enough proximity to Planet Earth to facilitate their arrival here, in search of something, - or for whatever reason? Perhaps like our modern-day beliefs about the possibility of humans colonising the Planet Mars? Certainly, when the first humans arrived on the surface of the Moon in 1969, there was evidence of mining equipment and machinery already established there. Evidence which has been kept secret and not for human consumption! Extraterrestrial races traversing through time and space? Who knows?

Sitchin's argument was that *'the past holds the key to the future'*. In other words, and as he himself put it, - *'To know the future, study the past.'*

So here we are left pondering, wondering and considering so many

'What ifs?' - What if all this information scribed on the ancient tablets is indeed true? What if all the *'stories'* are true? What if all the information reported on the ancient tablets really did happen? What if those ancient Sumerians were simply writing the history of those who went before them, - thousands of years before them, - just as we today write about the ancient Egyptians, the pyramids, the ancient gods and goddesses, etc. etc. etc ? What if those space travellers really did come to our planet from their own home planet Nibiru, which is believed by many to come into our own solar system approximately every 3,600 years, and brings its inhabitants within reach of Planet Earth? What if the Nefilim, - the royalty of their society, - and the Anunnaki, their rank-and-file, - really did come to Earth on their specific mission to save their own planet by mining gold here and transporting it back home? Or to colonise our Planet Earth with their own species? Again, - who knows?

Michael Tellinger is a scientist, researcher and regular guest on more than 200 radio shows in America, United Kingdom and Europe, such as Coast to Coast AM with George Noory and the Shirley Maclean Show. In March 2011 he hosted the Megalithomania Conference in Johannesburg, South Africa, featuring many of the top names in the Ancient Aliens programmes, including Graham Hancock, Andrew Collins, and Robert Temple.

In his book *'Slave Species of the Gods - The Secret History of the Anunnaki and Their Mission on Earth'*, published in 2005, Tellinger revealed new archaeological and genetic evidence is in support of Sitchin's revolutionary work with the pre-biblical clay tablets. He shows how the Anunnaki created us using pieces of their own DNA, controlling our physical and mental capabilities by inactivating their more advanced DNA - which, he maintains, explains why less than 3%

of our DNA is active. He identifies a recently discovered complex of sophisticated ruins in South Africa, complete with thousands of mines, as the city of Anunnaki leader Enki and explains the lost Anunnaki technologies that used the power of sound as a source of energy. Matching key mythologies of the world's religions to the Sumerian clay tablets stories on which they are based, he details the actual events behind these tales of direct physical interactions with '*god*', concluding with the epic flood - a perennial theme of ancient myth - that wiped out the Anunnaki mining operations. Tellinger shows that as humanity awakens to the truth about our origins we can overcome our programmed animalistic and slave-like nature, tap into our dormant Anunnaki DNA, and realise the longevity and intelligence of our creators as well as learn the difference between the '*gods*' of myth and the true '*God*' of our universe.

So! The ancient Sumerian clay tablets!

Chris H. Hardy, Ph.D, holds a degree in ethno-psychology. A cognitive scientist and former researcher at Princeton's Psychophysical research Laboratories, she has spent many years investigating nonlocal consciousness through systems theory, chaos theory, and her own Semantic Fields Theory. She is the author of many research papers and published books, including '*DNA of the Gods*' and '*The Sacred Network*'.

In her book '*Wars of the Anunnaki - Nuclear Self-Destruction in Ancient Sumer*' Hardy makes a strong case for the use of nuclear weapons many thousands of years ago. She maintains that the detonation of nuclear weapons in the 20th century was not the first time humanity has seen such terrible destruction. Drawing upon the work of Sitchin, the Book of Genesis, Sumerian clay tablets and archaeological evidence such as violent radioactive skeletons, Hardy reveals the ancient nuclear event that destroyed the Sumerian civilisation and the power struggles of the *'gods'* that led up to it:

'Archaeological excavations have unearthed the layer of the city streets in Harappa, and sprawled over these streets were dozens of skeletons of people that obviously met an instant death while running with their kin, some holding hands. Worse still, some skeletons, as was recently discovered, were highly radioactive, thus suggesting Harappa's dwellers had died during a nuclear attack. These skeletons have been carbon dated to about 2500 BCE.

Similarly, there are different locations on Earth where rocks of basalt, one of the hardest stones, have been melted by such intense heat and pressure that they have been vitrified - and the thermal intensity triggering the melting and vitrification process (in the absence of a huge crater that would have been left by a sizable meteorite) points to a nuclear explosion.' ('Wars of the Anunnaki - Nuclear Self-Destruction in Ancient Sumer', Chris Hardy Ph.D. page 4)

Hardy explains how the Anunnaki came to Earth from the planet Nibiru seeking gold to repair their ozone layer. Using genetic engineering, they created modern humanity to do their mining work and installed themselves as the kings and the *'gods'* of the Earth. At the start, the Anunnaki *'god'* Enki had a fatherly relationship with the first two humans. Then Enlil, Enki's half-brother, took over as Commander of Earth, instating a sole-god theocracy and a war against the clan of Enki and humanity for spoiling the Anunnaki bloodlines through interbreeding.

And in Hardy's opinion, two of Enlil's attacks against the Enki clan and humanity are described in the stories of the Deluge and the Tower of

Babel. Enlil's final attempt, after coercing the Assembly of the Gods into voting yes, was the nuclear bombing of five cities of the Jordan plain, including Sodom and Gomorrah, which resulted in the destruction of the Sumerian civilisation and the Anunnaki's own civilisation on Earth, including their space port in the Sinai desert. Hardy reveals how after each attempt, humanity was saved by Enki, chief scientist Ninmah, and Enki's son Hermes.

Nuclear War? In ancient Sumeria?

'The Evil Wind covered the land as a cloak, spread over it like a sheet.......an Evil Wind which overwhelms the land;......a great storm directed from Anu......it hath come from the heart of Enlil......like the bitter venom of the gods......bearing gloom from city to city.' (From the Sumerian Tablets and quoted in '*Wars of the Anunnaki - Nuclear Self-Destruction in Ancient Sumer',* Chris Hardy Ph.D. page 80)

Hardy explains how the Anunnaki's reliance on technology and their recurrent wars caused them to lose touch with cosmic consciousness. And she reveals how we will be doomed to repeat this dynamic until humanity awakens to our true origins.

The introduction to the book is written by Jim Marrs, an award-winning journalist and author of five New York Times Best Sellers, including '*Our Occulted History*' and '*Rule by Secrecy*'. He has been the featured speaker at a number of national conferences, including the Annual International UFO Congress, and has appeared on numerous national radio and television programmes. In the introduction, Marrs writes:

'It is not only mythology and old legends that give evidence of strange visitors - Viracocha to the Aztecs, Quetzalcoatl to the Mayans, Ptah

and Ra to the Egyptians, the Anunnaki and Marduk to the Babylonians - but also strange artifacts from around the world that provide compelling evidence that humankind has never been alone on this planet.'

So what exactly is this '*compelling*' evidence? Marrs give us numerous examples!

'The Antikythera mechanism, discovered in a ship by Greek divers in 1900, has been found to be a complicated astronomical computer of a sort. Electricity, thought to have been first discovered by Italian anatomist Luigi Galvani in about 1786, has been generated by a small clay vase containing a copper cylinder held by asphalt, discovered in Baghdad in 1936 and dated to between 150 and 100 BCE. In the center of this vase was a protruding iron rod tipped by oxidized lead. When filled with an alkaline liquid, such as freshly squeezed grape juice, the so-called Baghdad battery produced a half volt of electricity.

Other such anomalous objects include an exquisitely carved crystal skull found in South America displaying machine marks; ancient ornaments formed from molten platinum found in Peru along with a 2,000-year-old model of a delta-winged jet fighter; perfectly round stone balls found in Guatemala; stone cubes found in Iceland inscribed with ancient Chinese characters, and Cuneiform tablets from ancient Babylon that accurately describe our farthest outer planets, which could not have been seen without the aid of modern telescopes.

The list goes on. Individually, such cases might be explained away as hoaxes or misinterpretation of data. Much harder to explain is the existence of ancient maps that depict an accurate knowledge of both prehistoric geography and astronomy. Professor Charles Hapgood, historian of science, in his thoroughly researched book 'Maps of the

Ancient Sea Kings: Evidence of Advanced Civilization in the Ice Age', demonstrated that the Piri Reis map, dated from 1513 - shows the precise outline of thy Antarctic continent, at the time it was still free of ice, which Hapgood estimates was prior to 11,600 years ago. Yet, the Antarctic was first sighted in 1820, and only in the twentieth century was its rocky structure beneath the ice mapped by using sophisticated ground-penetrating radar. The ancient map shows the precise coastline of South America as well, which was not supposed to be known at the time.'

And the only conclusion that one can draw from all of this? Surely, as Marrs claims:

'It is clear that some group with advanced technology was active on our planet millennia ago. And it was not primitive humans.'

So we are forced to consider, - who were these ancient *'gods'* and how similar were they to us?

Marrs continues:

'This is where Chris Hardy definitely lifts a part of the veil. Her work highlights the very human nature of the specific group of ancient alien astronauts, known variously as the Anunnaki, the Shining Ones, the Nephilim - the sky gods. Those who state in their tablets that they were 'Anunnaki' - i.e. the ones who came down from Heaven / Nibiru (An) to earth (Ki).

Each researcher in the field of ancient aliens brings his or her own invaluable stone to the edifice, making the case of ancient high-tech people visiting Earth stronger and stronger. Chris Hardy's originality, though, lies in her precise analysis of very ancient texts, including

Sumerian, biblical, and Gnostic ones - the Sumerian tablets going as far back as 5,000 years ago, predating the Bible by more than two millennia.'

And Marrs draws our attention as to how too many identical events and similar psychological profiles of the actors/protagonists are described both in the Sumerian tablets and in the Book of Genesis to doubt that they both refer to our past. And among them?

'..........The creation of humanity in 'our image', the garden in Eden / Edin, the murder of Abel / Abael, the ten patriarchs / kings from Adam / Adapa to Noah, the Deluge and rescue of Noah / Ziusudia, the Babel / Babili tower / ziggurat, and not the least, the destruction of Sodom and four other cities of the Sinai and Jordan plains. And as far as these latter events are concerned, as Hardy shows, the very detailed Sumerian tablets give us clear evidence of the use of nuclear weapons.'

It is now time for us to look at the actual writings in the clay tablets! - Their account of the creation of humans and the very first modern human species that came into existence.

According to Sitchin, the leader of the Earth mission from Nibiru was Enki, the chief scientist of his race, and first to land on Earth, and it was Enki who proposed a solution to the labor supply problem when their own *'gods'* rebelled over the hard work required of them:

'We can create a primitive worker, a Lulu-amelu, somebody who will do this work for us'.

When asked by the Anunnaki leadership how he could create such a being, Enki replied:

'This being already exists. All that we have to do is put our mark on

it.'

Then the tablets describe how they mixed the genes of one of their young males with the egg of an ape woman, and after mixing the two, re-implanted fertilised eggs in the wombs of some of their own Anunnaki females who had arrived on Earth. And as Sitchin stated:

'The fact that I quoted it from the ancient text, that the fertilised eggs of the ape woman was reimplanted in the wombs of Anunnaki females who arrived on Earth, let's say the ancient astronaut females, has great significance to the nature of the being that was finally created; that is very important. And, as we are Homo sapiens, not the hominid race that came on earth through evolution, but we (a new species) appeared only about 300,000 years ago through the efforts of someone who jumped the gun on evolution through genetic engineering.'

So this is Sitchin's belief, - the end result of his spending his entire life translating and interpreting ancient Sumerian, Babylonian and Mesopotamian clay tablets, which, he believed were recordings of historical happenings. Not myths! But recorded historical happenings!

But before we look further into some of these ancient texts we first need to put all of this into context!

The Sumerian people arriving in southern Mesopotamia called themselves the *'black-headed people'*, joining other nomadic and semi-nomadic peoples settling between the Euphrates and Tigris Rivers and throughout the ancient Near East. It was these Sumerians who invented writing and later recorded the history, myths, and beliefs of earlier generations from oral transmissions, leaving all of it on their clay tablets, to be deciphered by later generations of humanity. The myths and legends coming from the ancient Sumerians are as numerous and as complex as the origin of the Sumerians themselves, and the variety and complexities of their different tribes, with all their hundreds of gods, goddesses and demons.

So what did they believe? How did they explain human existence and the purpose of life? And how did they explain natural phenomena?

Generally, they believed that the *'gods'* were responsible for, and had the power over all that happened in the celestial and human worlds, with humans there only to worship and serve these *'gods'*. These gods who were all related, - sons and mothers, sisters and brothers, fathers and daughters, all inter-marrying, and possessing the same qualities and emotions as humans, - all acting out of anger, kindness, betrayal, jealousy, spite, pity, etc. etc. etc.

Generally too, they believed that the Earth was flat, and enclosed in a dome that formed the heavens above and the underworld below. This was the universe over which the *'gods'* ruled, blessing and rewarding the humans with such as great harvests if they pleased them, or alternatively with punishments such as floods, fires or plagues if they displeased them.

So who were the main players, the main shakers, movers and makers in the story of Creation as told in these ancient Mesopotamian texts?

We have four primary *'deities'*, to whom the creation of the world and the creation of humanity were attributed, - An or Anu, the Father of the Gods; Anu's sons, - the half-brothers Enlil the Air God and Enki the God of Earth, Wisdom and Magic; and Ninhursag, the Mother Goddess. It was through these *'gods'* that the people understood and explained all human experiences and daily occurrences.

An or **Anu** was the primary god, father of the *'gods'*, the supreme ruler who maintained the entire existence of the heavens and the Earth, as the tablets tell us, '**the expanse of the heavens**'. Anu is depicted as a human wearing a horned headdress or a bull with a human head. Rarely the central figure in the myths, often in the background, Anu nevertheless gave commands to the other gods and goddesses, but in later myths we read about him ceding his power to his son Enlil and becoming even more remote.

As father of the *'gods'*, Anu was revered at the White Temple in the city of Uruk. The tablets report him ascending to earth as Nibiru approached Earth's vicinity, and one specific occasion was to resolve a dispute between his two sons, Enki and Enlil.

Enki, whose name first meant '*Lord Earth'* was the son of Anu and half-brother to Enlil. Enki was the god of the Abzu, and lived in the Abzu. Away back in the beginning, Earth was believed to be surrounded by an ancient saltwater sea. Fresh water came from underneath the Earth from an underworld sea called the Abzu, and this was where Enki lived. Enki, according to the tablets, was the first Nefilim to come to Earth and became known for his role as the Benefactor of Humans. He was the first-born son of Anu on Nibiru, but from a union by Anu with one of his six concubines, unlike his half-brother Enlil who, even though he was born after Enki, was nevertheless the product of the '*proper*' union between Anu and Anu's half-sister, hence Enlil's blood was more purely royal than Enki's. So both sons, each because of their own birth circumstances, claimed the right of inheritance from their father Anu.

Enki, according to the tablets, was responsible for purifying the waters of the Tigris river, and building a canal to allow a connection between the Tigris and the Euphrates rivers in their lower basins. Sitchin maintained that these hydrologic projects were Enki's efforts to control surface water inputs to the delta to alleviate the swamps, and as such they were feats of engineering that became so characteristic of Enki's dedication to making his own and the other Earth-based settlements of Sumer into thriving and sustainable habitats.

Enki was also in charge of the Moon, perhaps, as Sitchin suggests, because the Moon is related to tides. In his book *'The Lost Book of Enki'*, Sitchin gives us a first-person account of Enki's activities, - Enki relating his own narrative. Enki, - leader of the first *'astronauts'*, relating his own story, telling about mounting tensions, survival dangers and royal succession rivalries, explaining what life was like on their own planet, and the motives that drove them to settle on Earth.

But perhaps the two greatest achievements of Enki, again according to Sitchin's translations of the tablets, were his creation of earthlings by genetic engineering, and his creative way of saving a small seed of humanity in the face of the Great Flood or the Deluge.

In excavations at the site of the ancient city of Eridu, archaeologists have uncovered evidence dating back to about 6500 BCE. A temple which contained a shrine dedicated to the god Enki was unearthed, along with a water pool located at the main entrance.

Enlil, also son of Anu, was the air god, and the most important of the Sumerian gods, viewed as the most powerful and most formidable son of Anu, not just because of his birthright as Anu's most *'pure-blood'* successor, but also because of his leadership qualities and style. Sitchin explained Enlil's name as meaning *'Lord of the Airspace'*. According to the tablet records, Sitchin explains how Enlil was highly revered:

'Enlil, / Whose command is far reaching; / Whose 'word' is lofty and holy; / Whose pronouncement is unchangeable; / Who decrees destinies unto the distant future..... / The Gods of Earth bow down willingly before him; / The Heavenly gods who are on Earth / Humble themselves before him; / They stand by faithfully, according to instructions.' (Sitchin, *'The 12th Planet',* page 93)

The temple of Enlil, excavated in Dur-Kurigalzu, was a religious site where offerings of votive statues, rituals accompanied by music and singing would be performed for the god Enlil in return for blessings. He was seen as the god of winds, storms, air and earth, and it was believed he ensured that crops were nourished sufficiently and produced a good yield.

Ninhursag, also known as **Nintu** or **Ninti, Ninmah** and **Mammi** was a Nefilim born on Nibiru, like her two half-brothers Enki and Enlil. Ninhursa was celebrated as the mother goddess, one of the creation deities. And as one of the creator deities, she is the goddess of fertility, childbirth, and growth. She is also called the *'Mother of the Earth'*, the name meaning *'Lady of the Sacred Mountain'.* As the mother of the gods and the mother of men, Ninhursag is the most important female deity. All the myths of Ninhursag state that she had power over life and death, and in the myth of *'Enki and Ninhursag',* she can draw out or remove diseases and heal sickness. Depictions of the mother goddess Ninhursag often show her seated in front of a mountain wearing a layered skirt, either with her hair in the style of the Greek Omega symbol or with a horned headdress. Some depictions of her include deer, bison and eagles.

As the mother goddess, temples were dedicated to Ninhursag in many of the ancient city-states. Excavations unearthed temples in Adab,

Babylon and Girsu, where she was venerated under the regional names of Digirmah, Ninmah, and Emah, respectively. the Early Dynastic temple at Ur is dedicated to the goddess Ninhursag. It has an inscription on the temple that reads, *'Aanepada King of Ur, Son of Mesanepada King of Ur, has built this for the Lady Ninhursag.'*

Ninmah or Ninhursag was also known as Mammi, - hence the terms *'mother'*, *'mammy'* or *'mommy'* that we use today.

Marduk: First-born Son of Enki and Damgalnuna, or Damkira, and therefore grandson of Anu. M. J. Evans, already referred to, describes Marduk as:

'An egotistical Nefilim who made numerous decisions that caused all sorts of tribulations both for his family and himself....... Marduk rose to prominence in Egypt, where Sitchin surmises he was seen as the Egyptian god Ra. Egypt was Enki's domain, so Marduk's power there is understandable. However, that was not enough for Marduk. The information Sitchin gathers points to Marduk's almost uncontrollable ambition to gain control over Earth. If Enki, his father, had not lost his pre-eminent place as Earth's leader, Marduk would have inherited that role legally. His behavior tells us he believed he still was entitled to that birthright.' (M.J. Evans PH.D - *'Zecharia Sitchin and the Extraterrestrial Origins of Humanity'*, page 62)

And the subsequent wars between the Anunnaki leaders, in particular between the sons of Enki and the sons of Enlil is related in the clay tablets.

The two *'gods'* of Earth, both sons of Anu! Two Nefilim leaders, each called a god in the ancient cuneiform tablet sources. *'Gods'* coming to Planet Earth from their own home planet, and as we have seen, - for whatever reason!

Enki, seen as the merciful one who strove to save the newly created earthlings at the Great Flood, because he understood the value of humans as workers, - after all, he was instrumental in creating them! And Enlil, his half-brother, filled with hostility and intolerance toward humans. Enlil, who forced all the Nefilim to take an oath not to tell the earthlings about the coming Deluge, because Enlil wanted to eradicate the humans completely, seeing them as noisy, bothersome, immoral and gluttonous.

And so we have the *'God'* concept that developed and grew into later religious thinking and doctrine! Is there one God or more than one? Is God a merciful being or a vengeful one? When was the little *'g'* in *'gods'* changed into the capital *'G'* of *'God'*?

And of course the old question, - have we been made in the likeness of the *'gods'*, - plural, - or in the likeness of *'God'*, - singular?

So now, having identified some of the main *'deities'*, and before we delve into some of the ancient scripts, let us remind ourselves that we are inter-planetary, cosmic travellers, fluid nomads, journeying across time and space throughout all of the vastness of eternity and the depths of infinity in pursuit of soul expansion, - soul expansion through experiencing, experiencing, experiencing. Let us remind ourselves too, that we are not the only such travellers, and that our reality is not the only reality in the vastness of Creation. The cosmic, interplanetary, inter-stellar, interdimensional highway is indeed jam-packed! Countless civilisations, many of them perhaps millions of light years ahead of us in levels of consciousness, - civilisations we are unable to see with our very limited human vision. Just like the channels in your television set! They are numerous, but you can only see the one particular channel you are tuned into at any one time. The other channels have not gone away anywhere. They are still around you, just not visible, - because you are not tuned into them! So it is with other extraterrestrial civilisations and travellers, - they are above and beyond our scope of vision. But they are still there! And ancient peoples were much more aware of these other-worldly realities than we are today, - much more tuned into their existence. We have indeed lost our sense of cosmic consciousness!

And it is in these ancient Sumerian tablets, writings from mankind's earliest recorded civilisations, that we read about the idea of human beings originally being a slave race owned by an extraterrestrial society! So the idea is not a new one, not by any means! The Sumerians have left clear evidence in their records stating that humanlike creatures of extraterrestrial origin had ruled early human society as Earth's first monarchs. These alien people were often thought of as *'gods'*, some of them said to travel into the skies and through the heavens in flying *'globes'*, rocketlike vehicles and *'chariots'*. Ancient carvings, as already explained in Chapter 2 of this book, depict several *'gods'* wearing apparatus similar to that worn by modern astronauts.

The extant texts of the creation myth all carry the same basic story. The same basic story of how these human-like *'gods'* inhabited Earth in the beginning. An advanced civilisation, inter-planetary travelers, traversing through time and space! When they ascended down to Earth, there was a lot of work that needed to be done. The gods worked hard, making the ground habitable by mining minerals and toiling in the soil to make the land arable to produce crops. After some time, the *'human-like gods'* became annoyed and aggravated by the vast amount of hard work, and complained to the father of the *'gods'*, Anu. Anu agreed and listened to the advice of his son, Enki, who proposed that they create humans who could toil the earth instead of the *'gods'*. Together, Enki and his sister Ninki killed a lesser *'god'* and mixed his blood with clay from the fertile soil of the Earth to create the first human. These new beings were unable to reproduce, but Enki and Ninki modified the new being so he could function independently without the help of the *'gods'*. They called this man Adapa. This angered Enlil, Enki's half-brother, as he was not consulted. A conflict between the two half brothers erupted. Enlil became Man's biggest adversary. He put mankind through suffering and hardships. Since he was the god of the air, wind and earth, he could create droughts and floods.

So all of these ancient texts tell of man being created by the *'gods'*, beings from those other vibrational energy frequency levels, travelling through time and space and arriving on Planet Earth.

The Epic of Atrahasis

The *'Epic of Atrahasis'* is an eighteenth century **BCE** Akkadian epic, named after its human hero, Atra-Hasis. This may well be the most important of all ancient texts. It contains both a creation myth, explaining how the gods created humankind and an early flood account which was later incorporated into the *'Epic of Gilgamesh'* and is also thought to have influenced the biblical flood story of Noah and the Ark. It is also almost identical to an older story, the *'Eridu Genesis'* fragments of which have only recently been uncovered. In real life the flood itself was likely caused by natural, local events, the Tigris and Euphrates rivers being prone to flooding, but the story shows it being of epic proportions. King Atrahasis himself is listed in the *'Sumerian King List'* – exhibit WB44 in the museum in Oxford - as one of the monarchs who lived before the deluge or great flood, but his historicity cannot otherwise be confirmed or verified. This *'Sumerian King List'* testifies to those gods or kings living very long lives, sometimes for centuries.

The oldest known copy of the *'Epic of Atrahasis'* can be dated by its scribal identification to the reign of Hammurabi's great-grandson, Ammi-Saduqa (1646–1626 B.C.E.), but also various Old Babylonian fragments exist. It was discovered in Nippur, a city in ancient Mesopotamia, that was founded around 5000 BCE. The story continued to be copied into the first millennium BCE. The Atrahasis story also exists in a later fragmentary Assyrian version, the first one having been discovered in the library of Ashurbanipal. The best surviving text of the Atrahasis epic is written on three tablets in Akkadian, the language of ancient Babylon.

The *'Atrahasis Myth'* tells the story of how, following the creation of the earth but before the first human beings, the *'gods'* worked on the land, digging out the Euphrates and Tigris riverbeds, laying the foundation for cities. The *'Sumerian King List'*, in the opening statement says:

'When kingship was lowered from heaven, kingship was in Eridu.'

Both the *'Sumerian King List'* and *'Eridu Genesis'* tablets claim that Eridu was the first city on Earth where kingship was lowered to. What kingship? - Kingship of the *'gods'*! Replace the word *'gods'* with *'extraterrestrials', 'aliens', 'other-worldly travellers'* and we get the idea!

The cuneiform tablets discuss these first cities in detail, as well as the kings who were **chosen** to rule there. The *'Eridu Genesis'* Tablet states:

'When the royal scepter was coming down from heaven, / the august

crown and the royal throne being already down from heaven, / the king regularly performed to perfection the august divine services and offices, / and laid the bricks of those cities in pure spots.

The firstling of the cities, Eridu, she gave to the leader Nudimmud, / the second, Bad-Tibira, she gave to the Prince and the Sacred One, / the third, Larak, she gave to Pahilsag, / the fourth, Sippar, she gave to the gallant Utu, / the fifth, Suruppak, she gave to Ansud.'

Tablet I of the *'Epic of Atrahasis'* contains a detailed creation description about the Sumerian gods Anu, Enlil, and Enki, the gods of heaven, earth/sky, and water, and what the ancient people of Mesopotamia believed to be the true origin of mankind, as well as the true identity of who those *'gods of the Apsu'* really were:

'When the gods instead of man / Did the work, bore the loads, / The gods' load was too great, / The work too hard, the distress too much.'

Here is described, very clearly, in a time before man was created, how the lesser *'gods'*, - beings from other-worldly planets, who had come to Planet Earth, lived lives of endless drudgery, and were not at all happy with their miserable lot. A solution was needed!

'They took and cast the lots; the gods made the division. / Anu went up to the sky, and Enlil took the earth for his people. / The bolt which bars the sea was assigned to far-sighted Enki. / When Anu had gone up to the sky, / And the gods of the Apsu had gone below, / The Anunnaki of the sky made the Igigi bear the workload. / The Igigi had to dig out canals, / Had to clear channels, the lifelines of the land. / For 3,600 years they bore the excess. / Hard work, night and day, / They groaned and blamed each other, / Come, let us carry Enlil, / The

counselor of the gods, the warrior, from his dwelling. / And get him to relieve us of our hard work! / Now, cry battle! / Let us mix fight with battle! / The Igigi set fire to their tools, / Put aside their spades for fire.

When they reached the gate of warrior Enlil's dwelling, / It was night, the middle watch, / Ekur was surrounded, Enlil had not realized.

Enlil sent for Anu to be brought down to him, /Enki was fetched into his presence, / Anu, king of the sky was present, / Enki, king of the Apsu attended. / All the great Anunnaki were present.

The Igigi declared, / 'Every single one of us declared war! / We have put a stop to the digging. / The load is excessive, it is killing us!

Anu made his voice heard and spoke to the gods his brothers, / 'What are we complaining of? / Their work was indeed too hard, their trouble was too much.'

Ea (Enki) made his voice heard and spoke; / 'Let us create a mortal man / So that he may bear the yoke, the work of Enlil. / Let man bear the load of the gods.'

Nintu made her voice heard and spoke; / 'On the first, seventh, and fifteenth of the month / I shall make a purification by washing. / Then one god should be slaughtered. / Then a god and a man will be mixed together in clay. / Let a ghost (spirit/soul) come into existence from the god's flesh / And let the ghost exist so as not to forget the slain god.'

So what we can take from this Tablet 1 of the *'Epic of Atrahasis'* is that in the beginning, human-like *'gods',* in reality an extraterrestrial civilisation, inhabited Earth, with the lesser *'gods'* amongst them doing all the hard work of mining and extracting from the Earth all the minerals and resources the *'gods'* needed for their survival. After some sort of casting of lots, heaven was ruled by Anu, earth by Enlil, and the freshwater sea, - the Apsu, - by Enki. The Anunnaki, Anu's gods of the sky made the junior *'gods',* the Igigi do all the hard manual farm labor work of digging and maintaining the canals and water channels, but after 3,600 years they rebelled and refused to do any more hard labor. Enlil demanded to know who was responsible for the rebellion, that they should be duly punished. But his half-brother Enki, the god of the waters, advised against punishing the rebels, and suggested that humans be created to do the work. The mother goddess, the womb goddess, Ninhursag / Nintu/ Ninmah/ Mammi, was assigned the task of creating humans. A task accomplished by mixing clay with the blood of a junior *'god'* who was killed as a sacrifice. Hence humanity was created by mixing the blood and flesh of the *'gods'* with the clay from the Earth. - Bioengineering? Genetic manipulation?

However, it appears that Earth soon became overpopulated by this new human, and in Tablet 2 of the *'Epic of Atrahasis'* we read of how troublesome and bothersome these humans became to the *'gods'*. Tired of the incessant noise, Enlil sent plague, famine, and drought at intervals of 1200 years to reduce the population:

'600 years, less than 600 passed / The country became too wide, the people too numerous / Enlil grew restless at their racket, listening to their noise. / He addressed the great gods, / 'The noise of mankind has become too much, / I am losing sleep over their racket. / Give the order that suruppu-disease shall break out. / Cut off food supplies to the people! / Let the vegetation be too scant for their hunger!'

And in an alternative version in another text we read:

'Twelve hundred years had not yet passed / When the land extended and the peoples multiplied. / The land was bellowing like a bull, / The gods got disturbed with their uproar. / Enlil (half-brother and rival of Enki) heard their noise / And addressed the great gods. / 'The noise of the mankind has become too intense for me. / With their uproar I am deprived of sleep. / Cut off the supplies for the peoples, / Let there be a scarcity of plant-life to satisfy their hunger. / Adad (another Custodian) should withhold his rain, / And below, the flood, (the regular flooding of the land which made it fertile) should not come up from the abyss. / Let the wind blow and parch the ground, / Let the clouds thicken but not release a downpour / Let the fields diminish their yields / ....There must be no rejoicing amongst them.'

And in yet another tablet we read:

" *'Command that there be a plague, / Let Namtar diminish their noise. / Let disease, sickness, plague and pestilence / Blow upon them like a tornado.' / They commanded and there was plague / Namtar diminished their noise. / Disease, sickness, plague and pestilence / Blew upon them like a tornado.*"

Ghastly conditions indeed described here, where food supplies were cut off, diseases that affected wombs and prevented childbirth laid upon the people, and starvation becoming rampant. Lesser diseases and ailments, such as our equivalent of influenza were also visited upon humanity, suggesting that the Custodial *'gods'* understood and engaged in biological warfare.

Ring any bells? - Today's world! Fires, floods, earthquakes, natural cataclysmic disasters, food shortages! Are we indeed in some sort of repetitive cycle? - One can only speculate!

Tablet 2 of the '*Epic of Atrahasis*' continues:

'When the sixth year arrived, / Only one or two households were left. / The people's looks were changed by starvation. / Their faces were covered in scabs like malt. / They stayed alive by holding onto life.

Enlil became furious and fetched Enki / 'We, the great Anunna, all of us / Agreed together on a plan. / Anu and Adad were to guard above, / I, Enlil was to guard the Earth below. / Where you went (Enki), you were to undue the chain and set us free.

You were in charge of control and holding the balance. / But instead you gave wisdom and knowledge to the people. / Your creations have become too numerous and despoiled the Earth.

You imposed your loads on man, / You bestowed noise on mankind, / You slaughtered a god together with his intelligence, / Let us make far-sighted Enki swear an oath to the end, / To create a flood on Earth to wipe away all of life.'/

Enki spoke to his brother gods, / 'Why should you make me swear an oath? / Why should I use my power against the people? / That is Enlil's kind of work!'

Enki, who often takes the side of mankind in Babylonian mythology, intervened to help humans stave off these disasters. When Enlil instituted widespread starvation, Enki, who controlled the waters, foiled his plan by letting loose large quantities of fish to feed the people. Tablet 2 is badly damaged, but ends with Enlil's decision to destroy mankind altogether with a flood, and Enki bound by an oath to keep the plan secret. When all the previous measures failed to sufficiently reduce the population, a flood was decided upon, to destroy the human race entirely.

And in Tablet 3 we read about Atrahasis and the flood, a story also reported in *'Genesis'* and the *'Epic of Gilgamesh',* amongst other ancient texts. But this story of the flood in the ancient Sumerian texts predates the same story in Genesis!

In the tale of Atrahasis surviving the flood, as in both the biblical story of Noah and the Ark, and in the Gilgamesh tale of Utnapishtim, apart from the differing names, there are strong similarities and parallels. And this can only be explained by the fact that the tale of Noah and the Ark as related in Genesis, and the tale of Utnapishtin as related in Gilgamesh are both taken from the ancient Mesopotamian tale of Atrahasis. The later biblical writers simply altered the names and changed the many *'gods'* of the original ancient Mesopotamian writings into the one *'God'* of the Hebrew religion.

And then of course we have the biblical tale of Adam and Eve in the Garden of Eden. A tale that is unique in that it is entirely symbolic. Adam symbolises the first man, created by *'God'* from the *'dust of the earth'*. This strongly clearly reflects the earlier original ancient Mesopotamian tale that man was created partially from the *'clay'* of the earth and partially from the flesh and blood of the slaughtered *'god'*.

And where was the biblical Garden of Eden located? - In the Tigris-Euphrates region of Mesopotamia! - Surprise, surprise!

Tablet 3 of the *'Epic of Atrahasis'* tells us:

'There was once one named Atrahasis / Whose ear was open to his god Enki. / He would speak with his god / And his god would speak with him.

Enki made his voice heard to Atrahasis; / Dismantle the house, build a boat, / Reject possessions, and save living things. / the boat you will build, / Roof it like the Apsu, / So that the sun cannot see inside it. / Make upper decks and lower decks. / The tackle must be very strong, / The bitumen strong, to give strength.'

Atrahasis received the message and gathered the elders. / Everything was completed as instructed, / Atrahasis put all of his family on board. / Then the face of the weather changed. / Rain bellowed from the clouds, / Bitumen was brought to seal the door.

The winds were raging as Atrahasis cut the rope to release the boat. / Then the flood came and no one could see anyone else. / They could not be recognized in the catastrophe./ The Flood roared like a bull, / Like a wild ass screaming, the winds howled / The darkness was total, there was no sun. / For seven days and seven nights / The torrent, storm and flood came on.

The goddess Mami watched and wept / 'However could I, in the assembly of the gods, Have ordered such destruction on them?'

Nintu was wailing; / 'I have seen, and wept over them! / Shall I ever finish weeping for them?'

After the noise of the flood had subsided, / The warrior Enlil spotted the boat of Atrahasis. / He was furious!

'We the great Anunna, all of us / Agreed together on an oath! / No form of life should have escaped! / How did any man survive the *catastrophe?'*

Anu made his voice heard and spoke to the warrior Enlil, / 'Who but Enki would do this?'

Enki made his voice heard and spoke to the great gods, / 'I did it, in defiance of you! / I made sure life was preserved. / Exact your punishment from the sinner, and whoever contradicts your order.'

So here we have again, the same story of how human overpopulation soon became a problem. And how Enlil sent various disasters to diminish humankind, but Enki persistently foiled his plans. Finally, Enlil determined to send a flood to kill all humans, and the clever Enki devised a way to warn Atrahasis of the plan, without technically breaking the oath of the *'gods'* to keep everything secret from the humans. Enki advises Atrahasis to dismantle his house and build a boat to escape the flood. Atrahasis then built a boat and saved his family and animals. Enlil was furious at Enki for ruining his plan, but they agreed to devise a new way to control human population. Nintu arranged that one out of every three children born would die, and certain priestesses would be celibate.

The 'Enuma Elish'

And the ancient text, the tablets of *'Enuma Elish'*, known as the *'Seven Tablets of Creation',* also carries this same story of the creation of man. In Tablet 6 of this Babylonian Creation Myth we read:

'They bound him, holding him before Ea. / They inflicted the penalty on him and severed his blood-vessels. / From his blood he, Ea created mankind. / On whom he imposed the service of the gods, and

set the gods free / After the wise Ea had created mankind / And had imposed the service of the gods upon them - / That task is beyond comprehension / The gods were then divided, / All the Anunnaki into upper and lower groups. / He assigned 300 in the heavens to guard the decrees of / Anu and appointed them as a guard.'

Now the work previously done by the lesser *'gods'* was being done by this new human:

'With picks and spades, they (human beings) built the shrines, / They built the big canal banks, / For food for the people, for the / sustenance of (the gods).'

The *'Enuma Elish'* relates also the account of the war between Marduk, - son of Enki and grandson of Anu, and champion of the young gods, - and Tiamat, leader of the old gods. This Babylonian creation myth describes in Tablet VI how Marduk, after defeating the goddess Tiamat, commanded Ea to create man *'on whom the toil of the gods will be laid so they may rest.'*

Here we read about how Marduk gained dominance over the other *'gods',* created the earth and sky, appointed each of the six hundred *'gods'* to their duties, and oversaw the creation of humans. The *'Enuma Elish'* was composed at some point prior to the reign of Hammurabi of Babylon, 1792-1750 BCE, and found alongside the *'Epic of Atrahasis'* in the Ashurbanipal Library. It is thought to be a revision of a much older Sumerian poem. And many modern-day scholars, drawing clear parallels between Mesopotamian works and those of the biblical Old Testament claim that *'Enuma Elish'* strongly influenced the Book of Genesis. They would also however, point out that there are indications that these are all copies of a much older version of the myth dating from long before the reign of Hammurabi of Babylon

(1792-1750 BCE), the king who elevated the '*god*' Marduk to patron deity of Babylon. The poem in its present form, with Marduk as champion, is thought to be a revision of an even older Sumerian work.

The story, one of the oldest in the world, concerns the birth of the '*gods*' and the creation of the universe and human beings. In the beginning, there was only undifferentiated water swirling in chaos. Out of this swirl, the waters divided into sweet, fresh water, known as the very first '*god*' Apsu, and salty bitter water, the '*goddess*' Tiamat. When these two waters mingled, they created the other '*gods*'. In Tablet 1 we read:

'When the heavens above did not exist, / And earth beneath had not come into being —/ There was Apsu, the first in order, their begetter, / And demiurge Tia-mat, who gave birth to them all; / They had mingled their waters together / Before meadow-land had coalesced and reed-bed was to he found — / When not one of the gods had been formed / Or had come into being, when no destinies had been decreed, / The gods were created within them: / Lah and Amu were formed and came into being. /While they grew and increased in stature / Anar and Kiar, who excelled them, were created. / They prolonged their days, they multiplied their years. / Anu, their son, could rival his fathers. / Anu, the son, equalled Anar, / And Anu begat Nudimmud, his own equal. / Nudimmud was the champion among his fathers: / Profoundly discerning, wise, of robust strength; / Very much stronger than his father's begetter, Anar / He had no rival among the gods, his brothers.'

Almost immediately, however, and as we read earlier in other ancient texts, though with different names, Apsu and Tiamat regretted bringing the new life into existence, as these young *'gods'* were extremely noisy, troubling the sleep of Apsu at night and distracting him from his work by day. Upon the advice of his Vizier, Mummu, Apsu decided to kill the younger gods. Tiamat, hearing of their plan, warns her eldest son, Enki, and Enki puts Apsu to sleep and kills him.

And we further read how Tiamat, once the supporter of the younger gods, now is enraged that they have killed her consort. She consults with the god Quingu who advises her to make war on the younger gods.

And as the story continues, Enki and the younger gods fought against Tiamat futilely until, from among them, emerged the champion Marduk who swore he would defeat Tiamat. Marduk defeated Quingu and killed Tiamat by shooting her with an arrow.

After the gods had finished praising him for his great victory and the art of his creation, Marduk consulted with the god Ea, - the god of wisdom, - and decided to create human beings from the remains of whichever of the gods encouraged Tiamat to make war. Quingu was charged as guilty and killed and, from his blood, Ea created Lullu, the first man, to be a helper to the gods in their eternal task of maintaining order and keeping chaos at bay.

Following this, Marduk **'arranged the organization of the netherworld and distributed the gods to their appointed stations'** (Tablet VI.43-46). The poem ends in Tablet VII with a long praise of Marduk for his accomplishments.

Or so the story goes!

Both Genesis and *'Enuma Elish'* are religious texts which detail and celebrate cultural origins, but while Genesis describes the origin and founding of the Jewish people under the guidance of the Lord, *'Enuma Elish'* recounts the origin and founding of Babylon under the leadership of the *'god'* Marduk. Contained in each work is a story of how the cosmos and man were created. Each work begins by describing the watery chaos and primeval darkness that once filled the universe. Then light is created to replace the darkness. Afterward, the heavens are made and in them heavenly bodies are placed. Finally, man is created.

In revising the Mesopotamian creation story for their own ends, the Hebrew scribes tightened the narrative and the focus but retained the concept of the all-powerful deity who brings order from chaos. Marduk, in the *'Enuma Elish',* establishes the recognisable order of the world - just as God does in the Genesis tale - and human beings are expected to recognise this great gift and honour the deity through service. In Mesopotamia, in fact, it was thought that humans were co-workers with the gods to maintain the gift of creation and keep the forces of chaos at bay.

So similarities run through all the ancient texts! Even the setting is often similar! In the *'Epic of Gilgamesh'* for example, the *'gods'* lived in a beautiful garden, just like in the biblical Garden of Eden, between the Tigris and Euphrates Rivers. The name *'Eden'* itself is actually Sumerian and means *'flat terrain'.*

'Epic of Gilgamesh'

In the *'Epic of Gilgamesh'* we also have the story of the Great Flood, the Deluge, similar to that of Noah and the Ark in Genesis, and Atrahasis in the *'Epic of Atrahasis,* - from which large portions seem to have been copied or re-phrased. Just a change of names! In the tale of

Gilgamesh we have, not Atrahasis, but Utnapishtim.

The '*Epic of Gilgamesh*', in one account, tells, yet again, how the '*god*' Enlil cannot sleep because of the noise the humans are creating in the city of Shurrupak on the Euphrates River. The other gods agree with Enlil that the constant noise is just too much for them to tolerate, so they decide to flood the Earth and destroy mankind, - their own creation. The gods take an oath that they will not warn the humans, so all will be destroyed. However, and just as in other versions of the tale, Enki goes against the plan, warning, in this case, Utnapishtim, - Atrahasis in the '*Epic of Atrahasis*', Noah in Genesis, - instructing him to build a boat of certain specific dimensions, and to put into it his family and every animal on Earth, in order to survive the coming flood.

Adad, the god of storms in this same account, unleashes a terrifying storm, a storm of such ferocity that even the other gods are afraid. Ishtar, the queen of heaven in this tale, - Ninhursag / Nintu / Mami in the '*Epic of Atrahasis*', - cannot believe that she agreed to this terrible retribution. Utnapishtim offers a sacrifice of cedar, cane and myrtle, which he burns in a large cauldron on top of Mount Nisir, attracting the gods to gather round the sensual aroma. When Enlil arrives, he is angry that Utnapishtim and his family have survived the flood. Enki condemns Enlil for what he has done, and after conversing with the other gods, Enlil realises that the punishment he inflicted on humanity was too extreme, so he goes to Utnapishtim and bestows immortality on both Utnapishtim and his wife, as the first people of a new world.

The quest for immortality was indeed the main quest of all the gods, and it is this same quest for immortality that is the basic story in the '*Epic of Gilgamesh*', as detailed on twelve clay tablets, written in Akkadian and housed in the library in Nineveh. The hero in this myth is the hero-king Gilgamesh, king of Uruk. King Gilgamesh wanted Uruk to be seen as powerful and wealthy, and so he commanded the construction of extravagant buildings, magnificent ziggurats and temple towers, together with a defensive wall around his city-state, and agricultural lands and orchards. Gilgamesh was known for his strength, intelligence, and beautiful physique, believed to be two-thirds god and one-third human.

However, at the start of his rule, Gilgamesh was oppressive, tyrannical and cruel to his subjects, working them as slaves, constantly raping women from every class of society, and most abhorrently of all, claiming the right to sleep with every new bride on her wedding night. When the other gods hear the pleas of the Urukian people, and so learn of Gilgamesh's evil ways, they decide to create a man as magnificent as Gilgamesh himself, in order to tame him. They name this human Enkidu, and allow him to grow up in the wild amongst the animals and beasts, attacking shepherds, eating their sheep. uprooting their game traps and destroying their crops and fields.

And so a further plan was devised by which Enkidu could be tamed and transformed into a civilised man. A temple prostitute, Shamat, was sent out to search for Enkidu and to tame him, because it was believed in ancient times that upon union with a temple prostitute, such a man as Enkidu could be tamed and taught the ways of civilisation.

And so Enkidu became a part of civilisation and was taught by the prostitute how to be a rational human being. And of course the day inevitably came when Enkidu heard about King Gilgamesh's cruelty. So he travelled to Uruk to challenge the king to lay aside his evil and cruel ways and become a better ruler of his people. When he arrives in Uruk he finds Gilgamesh about to force himself into the bedchamber of a new bride, and so he places himself between Gilgamesh and the door, blocking Gilgamesh's entry. After a fierce wrestling match, Gilgamesh wins, but the outcome is a brotherly friendship between the two men, with Gilgamesh learning from Enkidu the virtues of mercy and humility, and working hard to be a better ruler for his people.

But as the years pass, Gilgamesh becomes bored and lazy, and yearns for excitement through new adventures. He suggests the two of them should travel to the Cedar Forest, a forest forbidden to mortals, to steal trees and defeat the evil demon Humbaba, - Humbaba being a devotee of the god Enlil, the god of air, wind and earth, part demon, part ogre and protector of the Cedar Forest. With the help of the sun god Shamesh, they defeat Humbaba. They build a raft from the cedar trees, and a huge gate from the biggest tree, which Enkidu plans to place at the entrance to Uruk.

After further exploits and adventures, King Gilgamesh and his new friend Enkidu sail back to Uruk. Enthralled by his beauty and physique, the goddess Ishtar tries to entice Gilgamesh into a relationship, and angry at his refusal, she asks her father, Anu, the great sky god, to command the *Bull of Heaven* to descend to Earth and kill Gilgamesh. The Bull of Heaven brings seven years of famine upon Earth, so Gilgamesh and Enkidu find themselves in a fight with the Bull in order to save civilisation. After a savage fight, the Bull is killed.

The killing of the Bull of Heaven, however, angers the gods, and they inflict a punishment on Enkidu of a disease, causing him to suffer from pain and hallucinations. His death throws Gilgamesh into deep depression and grieving for his friend, and causes him to begin to think about his own demise. Enkidu had told Gilgamesh before he died about his visions of the netherworld or afterlife, and now Gilgamesh begins his journey to the edge of the world to find Utnapishtim, the Mesopotamian equivalent of Noah in the bible story, and who we just read earlier, together with his wife, had been the only humans ever granted immortality by the gods - in this case, the god Enlil after the great flood. Gilgamesh is determined to avoid death and so never end up in the netherworld.

Gilgamesh meets up with a veiled female, Siduri the wine-maker who explains to him that he cannot avoid death, and that mortality is a blessing. But Gilgamesh is not for giving up in his search. Siduri shows him where to find the ferryman, Urshanabi, who will ferry him across the '*Waters of Death*' to find Utnapishtim. Gilgamesh finds Utnapishtim and hears from him how the great flood was sent by the gods to destroy all of humanity and how he himself was saved. He admonishes Gilgamesh, telling him that immortality would just take away the joy in life, as the inevitability of death is what puts purpose and meaning into life. Immortality is as much a curse as it is a blessing, and not something that could be accessible to just anybody on request.

Utnapishtim tests Gilgamesh by telling him that in order to gain immortality, he needs to stay awake for a full week, a task which proves just too much for Gilgamesh, with Utnapishtim explaining to Gilmaesh that if he cannot stay awake for just one week, then how can he expect to stay awake for all eternity? - Not a good candidate for immortality!

In the end, Utnapishtim persuades Gilgamesh to become the King that his people can admire. Utnapishtim's wife asks her husband to show Gilgamesh the plant that brings eternal youth, a piece of which

Gilgamesh takes and returns home to Uruk, with the intention of testing it out first on an old man and so prevent poisoning himself. But while Gilgamesh sleeps under a tree, a snake takes the plant, ending any chance Gilgamesh might have had of attaining immortality.

So Gilgamesh learns to content himself with knowing that he is not immortal, and his eyes are opened to the magnificence of the city he has built and the enduring achievements of the people. He will be revered for his building achievements and for bringing the lost knowledge of ancient times that he learned from Utnapishtim, back to Uruk. It is not attaining eternal life that is important, but creating an eternal legacy, leaving a mark on the world, - this is what grants a person true immortality. And so Gilgamesh came to be admired for what he could so for his kingdom and not for his heroic exploits and extraordinary adventures.

Chapter 6:

Ancient Babylonian texts

Myths and stories, yes! They abound in all cultures and all civilisations. And they all, - each and every one, - carry a message, a lesson, a moral, a hidden meaning which we are meant to find and interpret.

Descent of Inanna

The '*Descent of Inanna*' is another Sumerian poem written sometime around 1900-1600 BCE, which tells of Inanna, Queen of Heaven, travelling from the sky down into the underworld to visit her sister, Ereshkigal, whose husband had just died. The theme here and the lesson to be deciphered is one of injustice and the unfairness of life, with Inanna's bad choices leading to the suffering of others. Leaving the underworld, as the story relates, can only be done if the person's place is taken by another. Inanna however, refuses to let any of her sons take her place, as they are dressed in the clothing of mourning, believing her to be dead. But her lover, Dumuzi is dressed in rich clothing and jewels, and so Inanna decided it is he who will replace her. But before he can arrive in the underworld, his sister, Geshtinanna, the goddess of agriculture and fertility, volunteers to share his fate, each spending half a year in the underworld and half a year in the heavens. Hence it has come about that Gestinanna, being the goddess of agriculture and fertility, is now able to spend only half the year blessing the earth, - it was this bi-annual cycling that created the seasons.

Myth of Etana

Another Sumerian text gives us the '*Myth of Etana*'. The central message of this story is one of piety, of loving, and of course, obeying the gods! And so the main character had to be a well-known and respected individual. And that character was Etana, who, according to the Sumerian King List, reigned as the King of Kish in the third millennium BCE. The great city of Kish was created following the emergence of order from chaos and the birth of humanity.

Etana was considered to be the first king of Kish, which was a city located in the Fertile Crescent region of Iraq and Syria. According to the Sumerian King List, Kish was the first city on Earth that '*kingship*' was lowered to after the deluge. The reason the Legend of Etana is so important is that it provides a rare glimpse into the historical account of what occurred just **after** the events of *the 'Epic of Atrahasis*'. These cuneiform tablets explain how Enki and Enlil became associated with their particular roles within our reality.

The '*Legend of Etana*' was written in such a way as to hide its true meanings with clever parables and symbolic metaphors.

TABLET 1 Legend of Etana begins:

'They planned a city / The gods laid its foundations / They planned the city (Kish) / The Igigi-gods founded its brickwork / 'Let him be their (the people's) shepherd, / Let Etana be their architect....'/ The Great Anunnaki gods ordainers of destinies, / Sat taking their counsel concerning the land, / The creators of the four world regions, establishers of all physical form, / By command of all of them the Igigi gods / Ordained a festival for the people, / No king did they establish, over the teeming peoples, / At that time no headdress had

been assembled, nor crown, / Nor yet scepter had been set with lapis. / No throne daisies whatsoever had been constructed, / Against the inhabited world they barred the gates...../ The Igigi gods surrounded the city with ramparts / Ishtar came down from heaven to seek a shepherd, / And sought for a king everywhere, / Enlil examined the dais of Etana, / The man whom Ishtar steadfastly...../ 'She has constantly sought...../ Let kingship be established in the land, / Let the heart of Kish be joyful.'

This first tablet of the '*Legend of Etana*' describes how the Anunnaki (ordainers of destinies) had to create a new world after the destruction of the old one by re-lowering kingship to the city of Kish. Etana was chosen to be its architect and ruler since he was part of the royal bloodline of kings that can be traced all the way back to before the time of Atrahasis and Ubara-Tutu.

And the Mayan Popol Vuh creation myth also talks of the gods creating man:

'Let us make him who shall nourish and sustain us! What shall we do to be invoked, in order to be remembered on earth? We have already tried with our first creations, our first creatures, but we could not make them praise and venerate us. So, then let us try to make obedient, respectful beings who will nourish and sustain us.' (Quoted in Dennis Nappi, '*Food for Archons*' page 217)

Myth of Adapa

The '*Myth of Adapa*' is the Mesopotamian myth explaining why humans are not immortal. It tells of Adapa, the first man created by

Enki, being tricked into declining the gift of immortality. It bears strong resemblance to the Genesis story of Adam and Eve, where Yahweh banished the pair before they could eat from the Tree of Life. Indeed, keeping humans from attaining knowledge appears to be of great importance through many of these texts. And why? Possibly because by not becoming immortal, these lesser, mortal gods could be controlled and would be less able to challenge higher authority.

'And the Lord God said, Look, the man has become as one of us, knowing good from evil; and now, what if he puts forth his hand, and takes also from the tree of life, and eats, and lives forever?'(Genesis, 3:22)

Adapa, mentioned in several ancient texts as being the first man created by Enki, the god of wisdom, is a man of great intelligence and wisdom. But! Adapa is mortal, unlike other gods!

While Adapa is fishing, a strong southerly wind causes his boat to capsize, and Adapa raging and furious, breaks the wings of the south wind so that it can no longer blow. Furious over what Adapa has done, Anu the sky god, sends for Adapa, demanding an explanation. Before he goes to Anu, Adapa's father, Enki, takes his son aside and instructs him on how to behave before the gods. Adapa is told to decline all food and drink that he is offered, as it will be the food of death and a punishment for his transgressions against the south wind. But what Adapa does not know is that he has been tricked by his father Enki. And why has Enki tricked his son? According to the tablets, because Enki feared that Anu might offer Adapa the food of eternal life and so Enki would lose control of his son. And so Enki ensured that humans would never gain immortality. Anu, perplexed by Adapa's refusal to eat the food of life, sends Adapa back to earth to live out his life as a mortal.

And so it is with these ancient Sumerian, Babylonian and Mesopotamian myths! Those in this chapter are taken from the History Brought Alive series. And we have the lessons coming through very clearly! Lessons coming through very clearly that teach us of the origins of humanity, - creations of the *'gods'* and how the *'gods'* attempted to keep knowledge from the humans in case they grew too powerful. Also how these same *'gods'* punished humanity and how wars were fought between the various *'gods'* over how humanity should be treated, - some, like Enki, fighting on behalf of humanity in an effort to preserve the humans, and others, such as Enlil, fighting to control the humans and keep them in a servile condition.

Chapter 7:

The Emerald Tablets of Thoth

The '*Emerald Tablets of Thoth*' also known as the '*Smaragdine Tablet*' or the '*Tabula Smaragdina*' in Latin, is a compact and cryptic Hermetic text. It was highly regarded by Islamic and European alchemists as the foundation of their art. Though attributed to the legendary Hellenistic figure Hermes Trismegistus, the text of the Emerald Tablet first appears in a number of early medieval Arabic sources, the oldest of which dates to the late eighth or early ninth century. It was translated into Latin several times in the twelfth and thirteenth centuries. Numerous interpretations and commentaries followed.

Tablet 1:

'I, Thoth, the Atlantean, master of mysteries, / keeper of records, mighty king, magician, / living from generation to generation, / being about to pass into the halls of Amenti, / set down for the guidance of / those that are to come after, / these records of the mighty wisdom of Great Atlantis.

In the great city of Keor on the island of Undal, / in a time far past, I began this incarnation. / Not as the little men of the present age did / the mighty ones of Atlantis live and die, / but rather from aeon to aeon did they renew / their life in the Halls of Amenti where the river of life / flows eternally onward.

A hundred times ten / have I descended the dark way that led into light, / and as many times have I ascended from the / darkness into the light my strength and power renewed.

Now for a time I descend / and the men of Khem / shall know me no more.

But in a time yet unborn will I rise again, / mighty and potent, requiring an accounting / of those left behind me.'

TABLET 2:

'Far in a past time, lost in the space time, / the Children of Light looked down on the world. / Seeing the children of men in their bondage, / bound by the force that came from beyond, / Knew they that only by freedom from bondage / could man ever rise from the Earth to the Sun.

Down they descended and created bodies, / taking the semblance of men as their own. / The Masters of everything said after their forming:

'We are they who were formed from the space-dust, / partaking of life from the infinite All; / living in the world as children of men, / like and yet unlike the children of men.'

Then for a dwelling place, far 'neath the earth crust, / blasted great spaces they by their power, / spaces apart from the children of men. / Surrounded them by forces and power, / shielded from harm they the Halls of the Dead.

Side by side then, placed they other spaces, / filled them with Life and with Light from above. / Builded they then the Halls of Amenti, /

that they might dwell eternally there, / living with life to eternity's end.

Thirty and two were there of the children, / sons of Lights who had come among men, / seeking to free from the bondage of darkness / those who were bound by the force from beyond.'

Tablet 8:

'Far in the past before Atlantis existed, / men there were who delved into darkness, / using dark magic, calling up beings / from the great deep below us.

Forth came they into this cycle. / Formless were they of another vibration, / existing unseen by the children of earth-men.

Only through blood could they have formed being. / Only through man could they live in the world. / In ages past were they conquered by Masters, / driven below to the place whence they came.

But some there were who remained, / hidden in spaces and planes unknown to man. / Lived they in Atlantis as shadows, / but at times they appeared among men. / Aye, when the blood was offered, / for they came they to dwell among men.

In the form of man they amongst us, / but only to sight were they as are men. / Serpent-headed when the glamour was lifted / but appearing to man as men among men. / Crept they into the Councils, / taking forms that were like unto men.

Slaying by their arts / the chiefs of the kingdoms, / taking their form and ruling o'er man/ Only by magic could they be discovered. / Only by sound could their faces be seen. / Sought they from the Kingdom of shadows / to destroy man and rule in his place.

But, know ye, the Masters were mighty in magic, / able to lift the Veil from the face of the serpent, / able to send him back to his place. /

Came they to man and taught him the secret. / the WORD that only a man can pronounce. / Swift they lifted the Veil from the serpent / and cast him forth from the place among men.

Yet, beware, the serpent still liveth / in a place that is open at times to the world. / Unseen they walk among thee / in places where the rites have been said. / Again at times onward /shall they take the semblance of men.'

All declaring that negative, dark energies do exist! And that they do indeed invade our dimension! And Emerald Tablet 8 continues on from here to describe the *'reptilians'*, the *'serpent-headed'* that many believe are indeed controlling our planet!

And they are out to get us! Not with guns and bullets, but by mind invasion! Mind infestation! Playing to the ego! That's how they operate!

All fitting the descriptions many who have reported being abducted by alien races have given of their experiences!

Epilogue

The missing link?

Something big is currently happening in our world and to us. Something real big. And this real big is getting even bigger. A real big that can no longer be ignored, overlooked or denied. Unstoppable, undeniable, unfathomable.

But just how fearful are we of seeing outside of our very narrow and very limited view of what we think is our reality?

There is no doubt that what we saw previously as science fiction has now become science fact. So is all this science fiction-turned-fact telling us what **is** going to happen or warning us about what **could** happen?

Michael Tellinger, in *'Slave Species of the Gods'*, which we considered earlier, warns us:

'As we steadfastly march on the road to an unknown destiny, our ignorance has become our weakness and our arrogance has become a congenital disease threatening us with our own annihilation.........

The global population is torn between hundreds of religions and cults, all claiming to have the answers. Any semisober person will realize in an instant that they cannot all be right. Right? And yet it is religious dogma that has held billions of people captive through preaching death and destruction, threatening punishment by the 'almighty' to disobedient pilgrims, and promising reward and salvation to those who submit to blind faith.'

And we must remember! The word *'Government'* itself means *'mind control'*.

'The preface 'Govern' means to rule, steer, command and direct while 'ment' comes from the Latin word 'Mind'. We are so mind controlled that we don't even know or understand the true meanings of the words we use. This control is programmed into us from many different angles.' (Jason Quitt and Bob Mitchell, *'Forbidden Knowledge'* page 199)

So what about those 500,000 + clay tablets that have been excavated over the past 50 years? What about the true meaning and relevance of these same tablets, all of which has been identified by what Tellinger calls a *'handful of broad thinkers'* in the last 30 years? Those same clay tablets that describe ancient events, long before the bible was ever written! Those same clay tablets that prove that the stories in the Book of Genesis are simply watered-down versions of much older stories, those older stories conveyed in great detail in these ancient clay tablets!

'What was originally believed to be myth or fantasy, mainly due to ignorance by so-called scholars, has turned out to be documented historic evidence so fantastic that it shakes the very essence of our existence.' (Michael Tellinger, *'Slave Species of the Gods'*, page 2)

We have seen throughout this book how those who have studied the ancient Sumerian, Babylonian and Mesopotamian cuneiform clay texts have provided evidence that we, the human race, were created in the image of our creator, but that creator was not who we have been led to believe. The God of the bible and of many other religions, - the God with a capital *'G'*, - is obscured behind the mask of *'gods'* with a small *'g'*. Those *'gods'* with a small *'g'*, those extraterrestrials who ruled our

Earth with their own agenda in mind, punishing and demanding absolute obedience and servitude from their newly created human beings.

Tellinger tells us what it is that we need to do:

'....Uncover the slow and painful path the newly created human race had to travel and the crucial role played by more advanced deities who had ulterior motives for our existence...........Uncover the terrible truth that the human race was indeed created in the image of our maker, but the maker was not who we've been led to believe........ Unmask the god of the Bible and other major religions, showing the difference between God with a big 'G' as opposed to god with a small 'g'. The god who constantly displays humanlike behavior, the 'god of vengeance' we know from the Bible, turns out to be a god with a small 'g'. ('Slave Species of the Gods', Michael Tellinger, page 2)

Take the word *'gods'* out of the equation, and out of all the writings, and replace it with *'extraterrestrials', 'other-worldly beings', 'aliens', 'advanced civilisations',* - or whatever! And when we do that, we have a totally different perspective and understanding of our human origins. We have a new understanding of what Tellinger calls the *'Great Human Puzzle'*.

So, who are we? From where have we come? Where are we going?

Throughout this book, we have looked at the story of Creation as told in the ancient texts of Sumeria, Babylon and Mesopotamia, where civilisation all began, the main players being Anu, Ninhursag, Enki, Enlil and Marduk. All personified as *'gods'* but in reality, all of some advanced extraterrestrial race of beings!

We can interpret all of this in either of two ways, - either as historical happenings or as mythology.

And yes, myths and history make very uneasy bedfellows! But myths, legends, stories, parables - these were all the various ways in which writers long ago expressed themselves. And just like our present-day fairy tales and mythological stories and legends, they all carry within them a lesson or moral. Facts and historical accuracies are irrelevant in mythology. It is the lesson, the moral, the message that each carries that is paramount.

So what is the lesson we are being given from all these ancient texts? The lesson is that humanity has been created by the '*gods*'! - For whatever reason!

And how can we reach this conclusion?

Well, the stories are all telling us the same! The names may be changed, but the same basic story is running through all of them! And to repeat, - if we take out the names of the '*gods*' such as Marduk, Enki or Enlil, and replace them with such words as '*Extraterrestrials*', '*Other-worldly beings*', or even '*Aliens*', - then we have cracked the code!

Yes, the ancient Sumerian cuneiform clay tablets tell us we have been developed from the '*gods*'! Programmed by the '*gods*'! In the image of the '*gods*'! '*Gods*' being plural! Those beings who are depicted on so many ancient caves in so many different parts of the world, - descending from the skies in various types of vehicles! Our DNA has been manipulated in order to make us into the type of being those extraterrestrials wanted us to be! And according to those same clay tablets, after many failed experiments toying with our DNA, the required result was finally achieved! - A human being created by an advanced extraterrestrial race! A human being who would do the heavy mining and clearing work these *'gods'* themselves were unwilling to do.

In other words, according to the ancient Sumerian tablets, we humans came about through both the natural process of evolution **and** were created. The partially evolved being, Homo Erectus was used as the basic raw material, and genes from an Anunnaki were added to create the required being. Or so the ancient texts tell us!

'I will produce a lowly Primitive; / 'Man' shall be his name. / I will create a Primitive Worker; / He will be charged with service of the gods, / that they might have their ease.'

And:

'This being already exists. All that we have to do is put our mark on it.'

But! This newly developed being got too noisy, too troublesome, too annoying for the *'gods'* to tolerate. And so he had to be punished or got rid of! Hence all the tribulations of fire, plagues, diseases and hardships inflicted on humanity, ending with the great flood. Furthermore, these *'noisy'* humans were getting too smart, getting to know too much, and could possibly come to challenge the authority of the *'gods'*!

'And the Lord God said, 'Look, the man has become as one of us, knowing good from evil; and now, what if he puts forth his hand, and takes of the tree of life, and eats, and lives forever?' (Genesis 3:22

'Therefore the Lord God sent him (Adam) forth from the garden of

Eden, to till the ground from which he had been taken.

So he drove out the man, and he placed at the east of the garden of Eden cherubim (angels) and a flaming sword which turned every way, to shield the way to the tree of life.' (Genesis 3:23-24)

Forbidden knowledge! Knowledge which had to be kept secret and away from humanity! Or they would no longer be controllable!

Ring any bells?

'Evolution can explain the general course of events that caused life and life's forms to develop on Earth from the simplest one-celled creature to Man. But evolution cannot account for the appearance of Homo Sapiens, which happened virtually overnight in terms of the millions of years evolution requires, and with no evidence of earlier stages that would indicate a gradual change from Homo Erectus.' (Sitchin, *'The 12th Planet'* page 305)

*'Man is the product of evolution, but modern Man, Homo Sapiens, is the product of the **'gods'**, For, some time circa 300,000 years ago, the Nefilim took ape-like man (Homo Erectus) and implanted on him their own image and likeness.'* (Sitchin, *'The 12th Planet'* page 305)

" *'The Adam of the Bible was not the genus Homo, but the being who is our ancestor - the first Homo Sapiens. It is modern Man as we know him that the Nefilim created.......Enki [was] informed that the gods had decided to form an 'adamu', and that it was his task to find the means. He replied:*

'The creature whose name you uttered - IT EXISTS.' " (Sitchin *'The 12th Planet'* page 305)

And this '*creature*' that already existed? This was the hairy, naked hominid that walked about, ape-like, amongst the animals and beasts, indistinguishable from them, and like them, a product of natural evolution.

And did we not read in Chapter 5 in the '*Epic of Gilgamesh*' how the Nefilim '*goddess*', Ninsun, selected one of these '*ape men*' to be a companion for her own son, Gilgamesh, who was so troublesome? The '*Epic of Gilgamesh*', considered by many scholars to be the world's oldest piece of literature! Telling how Enkidu became the hairy, naked companion of Gilgamesh and was taught by the Anunnaki temple prostitute to let go of his '*animal-oriented*' ways and become '*civilised*'.

And the Book of Genesis carries the same report:

'And Elohim said: / 'Let us make Man in our image, / After our likeness.'

Note the pronoun '**our**'. - A plural pronoun. These '*gods*' were plural!

And after experimenting and failing many times to produce the creature they wanted, they finally succeeded. And so, - enter the human onto the world stage!

So that, according to the ancient Sumerian tablets, is our past! And what about our future?

It cannot be denied that humanity is at a very serious point right now! Our future as a species looks very doubtful! Has humanity, as we know it, run its course? Are we becoming more robotic and more machine-like orientated?

'Despite the 6.5 billion people who populate the Earth, the human race is a rather fragile and primitive species. No matter how intelligent and smart we think we are, we constantly display behavior that can lead to the decimation of our kind in the blink of an eye. We have waged war on our fellow man throughout history and continue to do so into the twenty-first century. There always seems to be a moral high ground or justification for our action. From Cain and Abel, to George Bush, it has always been the strong and powerful who oppress and wipe out the weak. The Old Testament of the Bible is not a pretty tale of compassion and forgiveness. In fact, quite the opposite. It talks about an eye for an eye; wiping out man, woman, child and beast in the name of god; and often mentions the enemy by name, personifying them as the bad guys or disciples of the devil. It seems that god has been taking sides from the very beginning. He had his 'favorites', and then there were 'the others'. ('*Slave Species of the Gods*', Michael Tellinger, page 4-5)

And the missing link?

The missing link, according to the Sumerian ancient clay tablets, comes from outer space!

Sitchin tells us that the evidence clearly indicates that **deliberate genetic modification** explains the appearance of modern intellectual humans on Earth:

'The tablet evidence clearly indicates that Homo Sapiens was a result of genetic manipulation by a scientific team from the space traveler group who came down to Earth and worked out the details of this design project some three hundred thousand years ago. ...We humans are here on Earth because the Nefilim needed our kind (intelligent willing workers) to rectify a labor shortage at their gold mines.'

And today, we too, - humanity, - we too are exploring space! Searching for other planets! Getting humans onto them! So is it so hard for us to believe that in an ancient past, other civilisations, much more advanced than us, and having much more advanced technology, were also travelling through space searching for the same thing? Is it inconceivable that just as we are exploring space and investigating such as Mars as a place for humans to colonise, - earlier civilisations likewise colonised our planet?

Is history repeating itself? Is the future to be seen in the past? And is our future on this Earth or in the most far-away reaches of the stars? Will we procreate with life we find on other planets? Will we create a new species? And will we be seen as '*gods*' as we descend from the skies onto our newly-found planet?

Have we been guided by extraterrestrials to fulfill **their** plans for us?

And finally! - A further point to consider! We saw in the ancient Sumerian clay tablets how these '*gods*' - extraterrestrials, - were able to manipulate the weather, - through creating storms, fires, floods, - in order to inflict punishment on their newly developed humanity. Too far-fetched to be believed?

But! We need only look at Operation Popeye, during the Vietnam War 1967-1972. Operation Popeye! A US military top secret weather modification programme! A secret cloud-seeding programme, whereby particles were sprayed into a cloud '*encouraging*' it to rain out. The hope was to extend the monsoon season, to bring heavy rainfall on the Ho Chi Minh Trail, which in turn slowed down enemy troops and flow of supplies, by softening road surfaces and causing landslides.

The former U.S. Secretary of Defense, Robert S. McNamara, was aware that there might be objections raised by the international scientific community but said in a memo to the president that such objections had not in the past been a basis for prevention of military activities considered to be in the interests of U.S. national security.

What did we just read there? - '……..*such objections had not in the past been a basis for prevention of military activities considered to be in the interests of U.S. national security.*'

The chemical weather modification programme was conducted by the US from Thailand over Cambodia, Laos, and Vietnam and allegedly sponsored by Secretary of State Henry Kissinger and the CIA without the authorisation of then Secretary of Defense Melvin Laird, who had categorically denied to Congress that a programme for modification of the weather for use as a tactical weapon even existed.

Buit a report titled '*Rainmaking in SEASIA*' outlines use of lead iodide and silver iodide deployed by aircraft in a programme that was developed in California at Naval Air Weapons Station China Lake and tested in Okinawa, Guam, the Philippines, Texas, and Florida in a hurricane study programme called Project Stormfury.

And of course, anyone who has been to Dubai or the UAR will tell you about the rain that falls from a cloudless, blue, blue sky! Yes, the Saudis can create rain!

So has our weather become a weapon of war? Has humanity weaponised the weather? If we could do it 70 years ago, as in Vietnam, then how much more capable are we of doing it now?

The truth is, - we just do not know what our governments and world leaders are up to! Nothing is surprising, shocking or unbelievable any more as those in power strive to further their own self-seeking ends, ambitions and agenda.

And just look at what is happening today all around us! Earthquakes, landslides, fires, floods, - all put down as natural cataclysmic events! But are they? And what about global warming? Is that a modern invention? A mere convenience for some sinister agenda?

In their book, *'The Cycle of Cosmic Catastrophes'*, Richard Firestone, Allen West and Simon Warwick-Smith present new scientific evidence about a series of prehistoric cosmic events at the end of the Ice Age. Their findings validate the ubiquitous legends and myths of floods, fires and weather extremes passed down by our ancestors and how these legendary events relate to each other. Their findings also support the idea that we are entering a thousand-year cycle of increasing danger and possibly a new cycle of extinctions.

No doubt, - there are alarmingly increasing numbers of people on our planet! And alarmingly ever-limiting resources to sustain us all!

Can we control the future? Yes, we can! And in a very powerful way!

Through the collective consciousness of humanity as a whole! If all humanity collectively could decide to live in peace and harmony with nature and to evolve into beings of higher consciousness, this would be the future we would manifest collectively. Those who can control the minds of humanity can control the future.

'Religion teaches us in order to be saved and to achieve ever-lasting life that we need to follow a particular religion. But the reality is for all conscious beings this power to have ever-lasting life is always within

us. Most of us just don't understand or realize this to be true.

Were not the biggest wars throughout history done in the name of God? Did not both sides believe they were all doing the will of God? How can both be right? How can both faiths be true?

But this is not the work of God. It's the work of power, greed and control. If a population gets too big to control, just send them off to war. If there are whispers of rebellion, start a war. The world has been in perpetual war for too long. We need to release these programs and choose to collectively come together to fight our true enemy - ignorance.

Media is the platform and narrative of this agenda. This is why we call TV shows 'programs', because this is what they truly are. It is programming you to the idea of what reality should be.

How you should think, feel and react to current events and politics, these are all staged and masterminded to follow a specific narrative and belief to push forward a future that is not our design. This is the matrix we need to unplug from.

This is the greatest fear of our controllers. If people took their power back, then the entire system and the reality they have woven would crumble.' (Quitt and Mitchell, *'Forbidden Knowledge'* page 201-201)

And where is the God with a capital 'G' in all of this?

'The simple answer and one that might take a while to understand fully or even accept is that we are all our own Creators. We are always connected to source and through us we manifest and embody the source.

The purest manifestation of this source is expressed through the energy of love.

Our creative power lies within our belief and faith, but through the programmed narrative of our controllers, we have turned religious organizations into the most powerful entities on the planet.' (Jason Quitt, *'Forbidden Knowledge'* page 200)

God is the Morphogenic Field! The Great Field of Consciousness. Grandmother Spider spinning her web of all life!

And as I have explained in many of my previous books, God is NOT a being of any sort! God is an energy, - **THEE** One Great Universal Energy that encompasses absolutely everything and everyone that is, that ever has been, and that ever will be. Nothing and nobody can possibly exist in any form outside of this One Great Universal Energy, this One Great Universal Consciousness we call God. And this One Great God Energy does not judge, does not forgive, does not punish, or do any of those things we have been led to believe. And why not? Because KARMA takes care of all of that! Karma! - The safety net built into our very existence!

So what does this One Great God Energy do then? This One Great God energy does just one thing! It creates! That's it! Nothing else! This One Great God Energy is a creating energy, - self promulgating, self-proliferating, self-expanding, self-everything. Expanding by experiencing **ITSELF** through creating! And we are part of that creation! We are part of that expansion! We manifest and embody the God Energy. We are the God Energy in physical manifestation. Just as are the extraterrestrials and all the other races and advanced civilisations that make up all of Creation. Our experiencing is expanding the One Great Universal God Energy! In other words, we are all **CO-CREATORS** within that One Great Universal God Energy! And that includes the extraterrestrial races!

As the late **Dolores Cannon** in 'Keepers of the Garden' informs us, through the information coming from one of her regressed clients:

'One must first understand what an extraterrestrial being encompasses. For it is common to perceive them as a physical being from another planet, which is accurate. However, there are many other forms of extraterrestrial beings. There are those in spirit form who are definitely from other planets, but yet are not physical, and these as well are extraterrestrial in nature. There are energies from other universes and galaxies and planets which are of such diverse nature as are human energies. All is extraterrestrial in being for all is of the universe. And as such, all is either extraterrestrial or none is extraterrestrial. There is really no delineation. There are, as in humans, many different forms of energies. There are in human form those energies which laugh a lot and have a very carefree and gay attitude. There are also in human energies those who are very serious and very somber. They simply choose to express their energies in different form. So it is that all energies throughout the universe are somewhat similar in this respect. There are many different kinds of energies in all parts of the universe and universes.' (Dolores Cannon, 'Keepers of the Garden,' page 171-172)

So, the Sumerian clay tablets, by all accounts, certainly offer a novel perspective on our dramatic and colorful past! Our dramatic past, where we see the chief of the 'gods', Enlil, not as we have been led to believe through organised religion, as a severe but just father, but rather as a despotic ruler who believed intermarriages between Anunnaki men and earthborn women were spoiling their bloodline.

And Enlil's half-brother Enki who saved Noah / Ziusundra, and thus humanity, from the Deluge, - whereas Enlil had schemed the utter destruction of humanity.

The struggles between the '*gods*', the extraterrestrials who first landed on our planet! And surely their story is **OUR STORY**!

All just too unbelievable, too incredible, too incomprehensible, too fantastical to be taken seriously?   -   Maybe so!

But then again......on the other hand.....?

When we look around us at what is happening in our present world..........?

Other Books by Eileen McCourt

Eileen has written 46 other books, including her first audio-book. All are available on Amazon. For more information, visit her author page:

www.eileenmccourt.co.uk

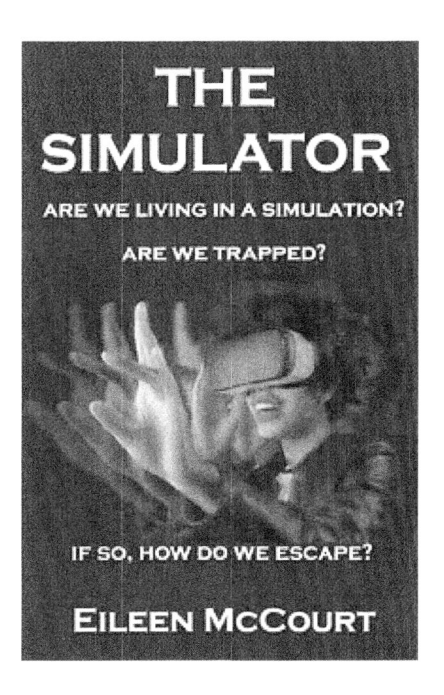

Other books by Eileen McCourt

Other books by Eileen McCourt

Dear God... Where Are You?
A Bewildered Soul Talks to God
Eileen McCourt

Changing Your Life - Living the Reiki Way - In Today's World!
"Just for Today..."
Eileen McCourt

Above Our Heads! Predators or Protectors?
Extraterrestrials! - The Best-Kept Secret Now Revealed?
Eileen McCourt

Finding Sense in the Non-Sense
Seeing The Greater Picture
Eileen McCourt

Other books by Eileen McCourt

THE SINGING SOUL -
THE RISE OF THE DIVINE FEMININE:
THE POWER AND RELEVANCE OF MARY
MAGDALENE IN TODAY'S WORLD
EILEEN McCOURT

LIVING EARTH
OUR RELATIONSHIP WITH
MOTHER NATURE
EILEEN McCOURT

MAN IN THE MIRROR
REALITY OR ILLUSION?
WHAT IS AND WHAT IS NOT
Eileen McCourt

LIGHTING THE WAY
A LITTLE MAGIC BOOK OF SPIRITUAL
MESSAGES AND MEANINGS
Eileen McCourt

Other books by Eileen McCourt

OUT OF THE DARKNESS OF DECEPTION AND DESPAIR - INTO THE LIGHT OF TRUTH
Eileen McCourt

PUPPETS ON A STRING!
BUT! THE STRINGS HAVE BEEN BROKEN! WE ARE FREE!
EILEEN McCOURT

HUMANITY'S GREATEST CHALLENGE?
ESCAPING OUT OF THE VORTEX OF IGNORANCE AND SUPERSTITION!
EILEEN McCOURT

CREATING A NEW WORLD
NATURE WILL BE OBEYED - THE GREATEST LESSON NEVER TAUGHT, BUT WHICH WE NEED TO LEARN
EILEEN McCOURT

Other books by Eileen McCourt

WHAT ON EARTH IS HAPPENING?
2020: YEAR OF BALANCE: RISE OF THE DIVINE FEMININE
EILEEN McCOURT

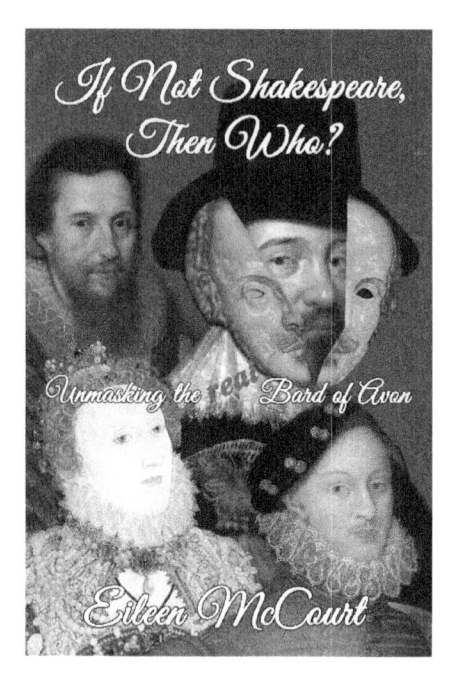

If Not Shakespeare, Then Who?
Unmasking the Bard of Avon
Eileen McCourt

To Be or Not to Be... The Man of Stratford Who Was Never to Be Shakespeare
Exposing the Deception That was William Shakespeare
Eileen McCourt

THE UNIVERSE IS MENTAL!
UNDERSTANDING THE 7 SPIRITUAL LAWS OF THE UNIVERSE, - THE HERMETIC PRINCIPLES THAT GOVERN ALL CREATION
EILEEN McCOURT

Other books by Eileen McCourt

Other books by Eileen McCourt

Audiobook

Other books by Eileen McCourt

CHAKRAS, CRYSTALS, COLOURS AND DREW THE DRAGON!
A child's second Spiritual book
Eileen McCourt

MUSIC OF THE SPHERES
Connecting to the Great Universal Consciousness and to ALL THAT IS through the music of Irish composer/pianist Pat McCourt
Eileen McCourt

RESURRECTION OR RESUSCITATION?
What Really Happened in That Tomb?
Eileen McCourt

BEHIND EVERY GREAT MAN...
MARY MAGDALENE TWIN FLAME OF JESUS
EILEEN McCOURT

Other books by Eileen McCourt

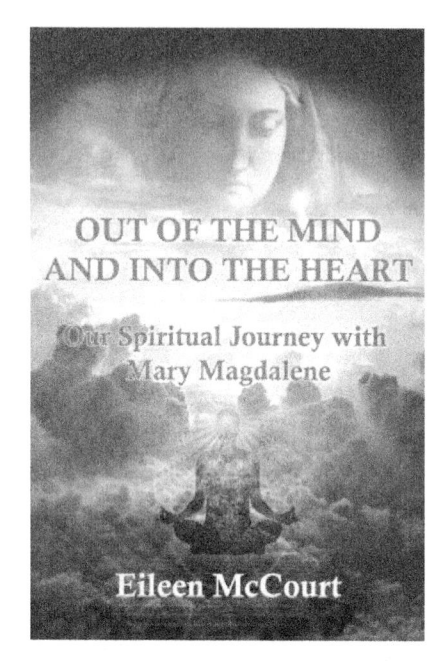

- DIVINELY DESIGNED: THE ONENESS OF THE TOTALITY OF ALL THAT IS — Eileen McCourt
- OUT OF THE MIND AND INTO THE HEART: Our Spiritual Journey with Mary Magdalene — Eileen McCourt
- JESUS LOST & FOUND: RESURRECTED FOR REAL 2,000 YEARS LATER! — Eileen McCourt
- Are Ye Not Gods? True inner messages and teachings of Jesus explained — Eileen McCourt

Other books by Eileen McCourt

- The Almost Immaculate Deception! The Greatest Scam in History? — Eileen McCourt
- ...AND THAT'S THE GOSPEL TRUTH! — Eileen McCourt 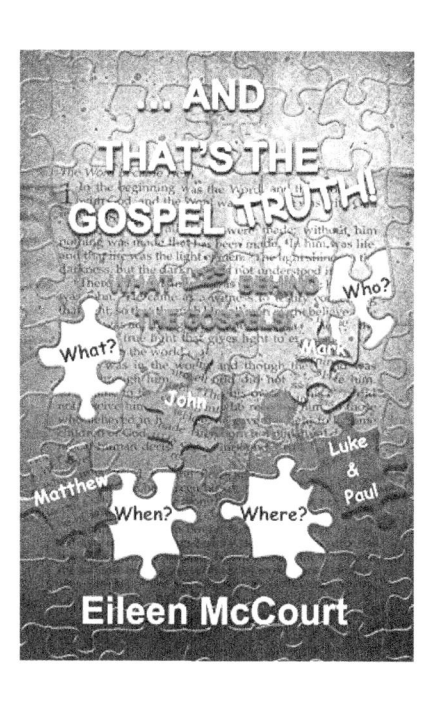
- Rainbows, Angels and Unicorns! A child's first Spiritual book — Eileen McCourt 
- LIFE'S BUT A GAME! GO WITH THE FLOW! A Spiritual Manual for Today's Teenagers & Young Adults — Eileen McCourt

Other books by Eileen McCourt

SPIRIT CALLING! ARE YOU LISTENING?
Eileen McCourt

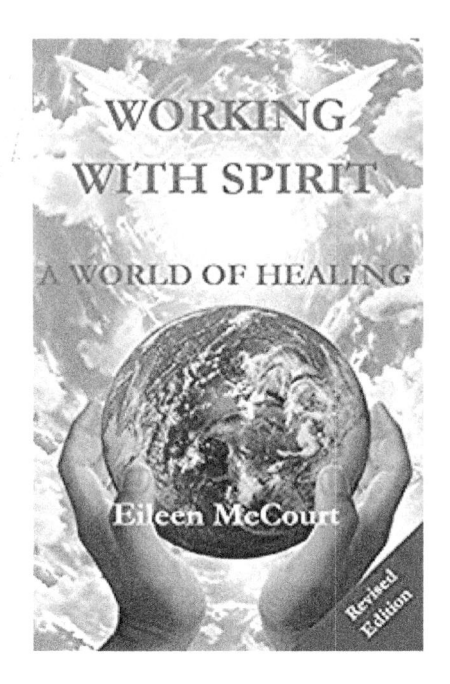

WORKING WITH SPIRIT: A WORLD OF HEALING
Eileen McCourt
Revised Edition

This Great Awakening
The part we all play in this time of our lives
Eileen McCourt

Living the Magic
Connecting the physical and spiritual worlds
Eileen McCourt